TINY LIES

TINY LIES

Kate Pullinger

JONATHAN CAPE
THIRTY-TWO BEDFORD SQUARE LONDON

First published 1988
Reprinted 1988
Copyright © 1988 by Kate Pullinger
Jonathan Cape Ltd, 32 Bedford Square, London WC1B 3EL

British Library Cataloguing in Publication Data

Pullinger, Kate
Tiny lies.
I. Title
813.54[F]   PR9199.3.P7/
ISBN 0–224–02560–0

Phototypeset by Falcon Graphic Art Ltd
Wallington, Surrey
Printed in Great Britain by
Mackays of Chatham PLC, Chatham, Kent

for John McNulty, Percy and Margaret Pullinger,
my family and friends

stories first published elsewhere

The Battersea Power Station, *Emergency* (1985)
Franz Kafka's Shirt, *New Statesman* (1986)
The Fact-Finding Mission, *Emergency* (1986)
The Micro-Political Party, *City Limits* (1986)
The First Mistake, *The Fiction Magazine* (1987)

Acknowledgments

I would like to thank Frances Coady, my editor at Cape, for her sharp eye and enthusiasm; Geoff Dyer for his encouragement; Pete Ayrton, Paul Gilroy, Vron Ware, Mandy Rose, Max Farrar, and Mark Ainley for publishing me in *Emergency*; Jonathan Shopley for his typewriter; Ellen Battle for the holidays; and Pam Baird for her support and friendship.

Contents

The Wardrobe

After her sister went mad, Josephine couldn't see the point in carrying on behaving normally but she tried not to think about this and went on with her life. She herself had very little propensity towards madness; she had always been the practical one in the family. It was Fin, her sister, who'd been the flighty one. So when Fin went mad, or rather, decided to stop pretending and do what she wanted, it was Josephine who bore the brunt of it. It was she who made all the arrangements, it was she who consoled the rest of the family, and it was she who put on the brave face to the authorities. Everyone, including her brother Arthur, was incapacitated.

What Fin did is something that many people toy with doing, or perhaps are afraid they'll do. She began by leaving her phone off the hook for days on end, claiming that the noise it made when it rang frightened her and she was sure it would bring bad news. She stopped reading newspapers, listening to the radio and watching television. Talking to her became difficult.

One morning Fin wore her pyjamas to work. Her boss sent her home in a taxi. Fin went back to bed but got up again later in the day and, still in her pyjamas, went for a walk along the river. No one is exactly sure what happened next but Fin was spotted on Lambeth Bridge at about 6.00 p.m., walking along in her nightclothes which couldn't have afforded much protection against the elements. Half an hour later she was seen in an inner-tube floating past the Tower of London. When the police boat caught up with her she told them to leave her alone, she had decided to take to the high seas.

'I'm fucking fed up with all this shit,' she said to the police officer who was frightened by the look in her eyes. 'I'm fed up and I'm damn well getting away from this place. Look at that,' she shouted, pointing in the direction of the City. 'It's fucking disgusting, all those goddamn banks, there is no morality anyway, no one gives a damn about anything. I don't trust anyone anymore. You're all bloody liars. The whole world is one big fucking Masonic Lodge, I know it.' The police officer held on to Fin's arm, leaning over the edge of the boat. He listened to her carefully so that he could make a report. In the end all he wrote on his notepad was 'She's a nutter'. Fin was condemned but she didn't care one bit.

A little while later after Fin was picked up Josephine received a phone call from the police.

'Are you Josephine Cutler?' a male voice asked.

'Why, who are you?' Josephine replied.

'This is Sergeant Bulk speaking from the Metropolitan River Police. We've got a woman here who claims to be your sister. She identifies herself as Fin Cutler.'

'Yes, Fin is my sister,' said Josephine, feeling she already knew what had happened. 'I'll be right there.'

At the police station an officer led Josephine into the cells. Fin looked thin and tired as she shivered inside her blanket.

'Josephine!' she said. 'Tell them I do this all the time. Make them let me go, Josie. What bastards they are.'

'Fin, sweetheart, what happened?'

'I was trying to escape, babyface. I was trying to get out of this hellhole before it was too late. I know, I know,' she said shaking her head, 'I should have taken you and

Arthur with me. But there just wasn't enough room and I had to get away. I wore my pyjamas so that no one could see me.'

'But, Fin, you can't get anywhere in an inner-tube on the Thames.'

'I could have Josie, if they'd given me a chance.'

A police officer cut Josephine's visit short so they could take her sister to the hospital. Over the next couple of weeks Fin told so many different stories that nobody wanted to listen to her any longer except Josephine and Arthur, but they didn't get to see her very often. Soon it was evident that Fin would have to stay in the hospital for quite a while. Whenever Josephine went to visit her she had some new escape plan.

'This time, Josie, I'm going to wait until it's really windy and then ask if I can go outside in the grounds with my kite. I'm light enough. I know I am. I haven't eaten for days.' Josephine shook her head slowly and on the way home on the underground she found herself in tears.

Still, Josephine carried on working and going to the pub and doing the washing-up. On Wednesdays she had dinner with Arthur and on Sundays she visited Fin. When she had a bit of extra money she would buy herself a new dress. Josephine had a closet that was full of clothes she never wore: black tulle, burgundy organza, dresses with hoops, lace. Brightly coloured long kaftans, shiny blue taffeta, a pink satin mini-skirt: Josephine's closet was like a secret garden that an invisible gardener culti-vated and no one ever sat in. She would stare down at it from her window, or rather open her closet doors and look at the colours without ever stepping into them.

Josephine had a whole list of shops she frequented during her lunch hour. She found nothing quite so satisfying as spotting a dress that she wanted. After circling around it for days she would finally gather up her courage and take it off the rack. In the fitting room she would stare at herself in the mirror feeling transformed. This was the only time she actually wore these clothes. A paisley frock with a bow at the back, a black cotton shift with slits up the legs, a crêpe-de-chine skirt with a contrasting top: Josephine spent a lot of money on clothes.

One Wednesday when Arthur was over for tea Josephine said to him, 'Arthur, you've been working so hard since Fin went into the hospital. Why don't you go away for a holiday somewhere? Take a break.'

'Me, take a holiday?' replied Arthur. 'But you need a holiday just as much as I do. Besides, I can't afford one.'

'Oh, that's nonsense. Flights are so cheap these days. You should go away to Spain or somewhere like that. Lie on a beach and go to nightclubs.'

'Josephine, you know I don't like the sun and I hate dancing. Besides, I'd worry about you and Fin. Who'd be here to make sure you're all right? Who'd visit Fin on Tuesdays?'

'But, Arthur,' said Josephine, 'you're too young to be so serious.'

'You should talk, Josefiend, you should talk. You're younger than both Fin and I. It's you who goes about with a long face. Fin and I are perfectly happy. I think you should go away on holiday.'

On Sunday, when Josephine was at the hospital, Fin said, 'Josephine, you look terrible. Take a holiday. Go away and get some sunshine. You worry too much. I'm fine,' she said, giggling. 'I tricked a nurse the other day. For three days I didn't speak. Not one word. Then just when she was getting really fed up with me I asked her which was the way to the nearest exit out of this place. I think she wanted to kill me. Anyway, Josie, you should take a holiday. I'm tired of seeing your worried face every Sunday. Give me a break.' Fin winked.

So Josephine and Arthur decided to go away together. They bought European train tickets and packed their bags. Before they left Fin told them where she had hidden her money when she ran away, so they took that with them as well. On the day of their departure they met at Victoria Station.

'My God Josefiend,' swore Arthur, 'your suitcase is enormous! What have you got in it?'

'Just a few things,' said Josephine quietly.

In Paris, on the Champs-Elysées, Josephine wore scarlet mousseline with a matching bow in her hair; in Lyons, crimson moire with a black beret. On a gondola in Venice she wore an olive gabardine dress that was double-breasted at the front and fitted at the back. Every morning, over the brioche and coffee, Arthur said, 'Wow.' Josephine had never been happier.

They travelled across Europe like two migrating birds, coming to rest wherever they pleased. In Vienna Josephine had to buy a second suitcase which Arthur did not mind having to carry; it made him happy to see his sister relaxed. They sat silently, staring out of the windows of the fast European trains, Josephine's hands folded neatly in her gloves. They travelled beside rivers and along coastlines. Josephine's wardrobe expanded.

After three weeks they returned home to their jobs. That Sunday they went to see Fin together.

'But, you've come back!' cried Fin when she saw them. 'You were meant to escape, not return,' she said, her voice full of anguish as she began to sob. 'Why? Why? Did they catch you? You weren't meant to come back. I thought you'd gone for me.'

Arthur and Josephine stood at the foot of Fin's bed. They were speechless. Josephine went up to Fin and attempted to put an arm around her heaving shoulders.

'Don't touch me!' Fin shouted. 'You could have gone! Now they'll get you too. If you can escape, why don't you?'

'But Fin,' stuttered Josephine. 'Fin. We had to come back. We've got responsibilities. We've got you.'

'No you haven't!' shouted Fin. 'They've got me. You've got no responsibilities except for those you've made up! You're mad not to escape. Mad!' Arthur took Josephine by the hand.

'We'd better go home Josephine,' he said.

'Yes, you'd better,' shouted Fin.

On the underground Arthur sat with his arm around Josephine. 'Maybe she's right,' he said.

'Right about what?' snapped Josephine. 'We can't stay on holiday forever.'

'No, but maybe we should leave.'

'Why?'

'I don't know. Maybe Fin knows something we don't.'

'I'm sure she does Arthur. She must do.' When they reached the next stop they said goodbye and Josephine got off the train. She walked up the street to her flat very slowly. Sunday afternoon was dead in London; everyone had bought their newspapers and shut the door. Josephine made herself a cup of tea then went into her bedroom. She opened her closet doors and stood looking at the colour of her clothes. Then she climbed into the wardrobe and closed the doors behind her.

Franz Kafka's Shirt

———◆———

Genevieve paid a great deal of attention to her dreams because she believed they revealed important things about her state of mind. Her dream-life was particularly rich; Genevieve could often remember her dreams with a clarity that she rarely found in her actual waking life. Her dreams were like little absurdist plays, one after the other, night after night. It was as if Ionesco had moved into her subconscious.

From time to time Genevieve's dreams were more straightforward, tiny snippets of wish-fulfilment that lasted five seconds, like the night she dreamed she was given a pen, the ink of which would never blot, and the time she dreamed she went back to school and humiliated the boy who once told her she was ugly. But, more often her dreams made little obvious sense and Genevieve had to spend whole mornings figuring out what they meant. She had her own set of dream-analysis tools, and her own ideas about the symbolism within her. Not for her the Freudian, Jungian, Reichian interpretations, nor even the more hippy ideas of dreaming and astrology.

Genevieve's dreams were like theatre, so she interpreted them like theatre. She enjoyed them and queued for ice-cream in the interval. She appreciated the art behind their creation, and she admired the design of the sets. Most of all, she was thrilled with the way she almost always knew all the people in the dream. It was like having a fringe theatre company devoted to the interpretation of one's own life. That was how Genevieve saw her dreams: very interesting, often disturbing, but something that didn't actually have much impact upon the everyday occurrences of her diurnal life.

In this waking life, Genevieve was a normalish type of person. She had a job she didn't like, although it didn't annoy her enough to make her look for another one. She had a pleasant social life and spent many happy evenings arguing with her friends in front of the fire. She went to the cinema, the theatre, the odd party, she wore lipstick in the evening, and she smoked too much. She fell in love and had her heart broken. And she had vivid dreams every night. Genevieve didn't feel there was anything particularly lacking from her own life, although many of her friends, with lives just like hers, did.

Occasionally Genevieve and her friends talked about their dreams. When Genevieve told the others about hers everybody laughed and said they wished they had such entertaining, strange, nonsensical dreams. No one thought there could possibly be anything wrong with the way Genevieve was dreaming.

One night Genevieve dreamed she was wearing Franz Kafka's shirt. In this very brief dream all that happened was Genevieve found herself standing on the pavement in front of where she lived. She looked down at what she was wearing and when she saw the shirt she had on, she knew that it was Franz Kafka's shirt. That was it. That was all that happened in the dream.

But the weekend after having that dream, and after Genevieve and her friends had had a good giggle at the absurdity of it, Genevieve went to a jumble sale. As she was looking through a pile of shirts on a table in the church hall she found herself holding a shirt that she felt, against all probability, was Franz Kafka's shirt. It was an

ordinary man's shirt of a variety often to be found at
jumble sales, cotton-mix, rather soiled around the collar,
and worn thin on the left elbow. The only remarkable
thing about this shirt, other than the fact that Genevieve
was sure it was Franz Kafka's shirt, was that it was
printed with a motif of beige cowboys on beige bucking
broncos. It was a discreet motif, the sort of print one
would not notice unless one really looked at that kind of
thing, like someone with a theory about understanding
men by examining the patterns on their shirts. Genevieve
was not that kind of a person.

Quickly, and not without exhibiting embarrassment,
Genevieve bought the shirt from the elderly woman
behind the table insisting on paying twenty pence instead of the ten pence for which the woman had asked.
She took the shirt home with her and soaked it in the bath
tub for the afternoon, hoping to remove the stain around
the neck, and also, even if she didn't think of it, hoping to
remove whatever it was about the shirt that made her
think it was Franz Kafka's. While it soaked Genevieve sat
in the kitchen. She told herself that Franz Kafka had been
dead for rather a long time, and as far as she knew he had
never lived in her neighbourhood, let alone her country,
and the chances that a shirt that had been anywhere near
Franz Kafka would turn up at a jumble sale in South
London were very slim. As well as all that, she felt quite
certain having read several of his books that Franz Kafka
would not have worn a shirt with a motif of cowboys on
bucking broncos adorning it, no matter how discreet.

Still, once she had taken the shirt out of the tub, washed
it, wrung it dry, and hung it up, and then looked at it
hanging there, rather limp and not even terribly stylish,
she knew that it was Franz Kafka's shirt and there was
nothing she could do about it.

So, she wore it. She wore it to parties, she wore it to
work, she wore it to the cinema. No one ever noticed the
shirt, except for a few people who laughed at the cow-

boys, and although Genevieve lived with the hope that one day someone would say 'Hey! Isn't that Franz Kafka's shirt?' no one ever did. Gradually Genevieve became accustomed to wearing Franz Kafka's shirt and the urge to find someone to talk to about it, an urge that came over her with particular strength when she was drunk, faded. All she was left with was a rather uninteresting looking piece of clothing, and a faint sense that something, somewhere, was odd.

Genevieve's life went on as it always had done and her dream-life continued as well. More miniature absurdist dramas took place in her mind than at any real theatre. These dreams continued to amuse Genevieve, and her friends.

Then, one night during the wet and bleak London winter, months after she had dreamed about Franz Kafka's shirt, Genevieve dreamed about swimming. She was swimming with Franz Kafka in a murky, muddy river. Franz Kafka was wearing a swimming costume, modern and brief in style, printed with the same pattern as his shirt, cowboys and bucking broncos. They were swimming the Australian crawl side by side when Franz Kafka suddenly stopped and shouted at Genevieve, 'What makes you think you can wear a dead writer's clothes?' Genevieve also stopped swimming and turned her body in the water so she could face him. 'That was my favourite shirt,' he added indignantly.

'Oh, was it?' said Genevieve. 'Don't you think you've been dead for rather too long to be complaining about this sort of thing?'

'Humph,' said Franz Kafka, cheekily, 'I suppose it will be my shoes next. Or, perhaps, Dostoevsky's underwear, eh?'

'Shut up,' Genevieve shouted, 'you're dead!' And with that, she lunged at Franz Kafka, travelling through the water like a torpedo, and grabbed him around the neck. With one hand she attempted to throttle him whilst with the other she tried to twist off his head. The expression on Franz Kafka's face was terrible.

Genevieve woke up when she felt hot water on her hands. At first she thought it was Franz Kafka's blood, streaming from his neck, but she realised quickly that she had unscrewed her hot water bottle whilst dreaming. She screwed the top back in and then sat up, dismayed to find a colossal wet patch in the centre of the bed, like the unpleasant leftover of a wild sexual tryst.

Genevieve did not sleep for the remainder of the night and she was not to sleep for the many nights that followed. Early in the morning she would rise, put on Franz Kafka's shirt and go for long walks along the Thames. From Vauxhall Bridge she would stare down into the murky, muddy water of the river. She half expected to one day see the body of Franz Kafka floating there, identifiable by his swimming costume, the faint pattern of beige cowboys on beige bucking broncos.

The First Mistake
or How To Read Marx

She tarted herself up for him. That was Isabel's first
mistake.

She agreed with what he said without really thinking
about his words and anticipated his jokes with a smile,
sparkling with wit, charm, and light. She said what she
thought he'd want to hear and she was usually right. Her
feminine intuition did not let her down, although it could
be argued that that very same intuition was her downfall.
Isabel expended a lot of effort in trying to please Archie.
That was another mistake.

Their eyes met at a weekend seminar on Marx at the
university. Neither of them had read Marx and, in the pub
at lunchtime, they both instinctively recognised each
other's ignorance. Archie picked up his drink and walked
over to Isabel's table. He had thick, black eyebrows and
big hands and feet. When he sat down next to her as she
sipped her beer coolly, she thought for a moment she
might ignore him, afraid she would be forced to confess to
not having read Marx.

'I haven't read it,' Archie said, without looking at
Isabel. He gazed out across the pub with a faraway look in
his eyes, then said, 'I don't have time to actually read it. I

23

know it through my bones anyway. Sometimes I think Marx is just in the air, something I breathe without having to think. He's just there.'

Isabel sat watching Archie as he spoke. He still hadn't looked at her. 'I know what you mean, in fact,' she said. 'I haven't read it either. I haven't read anything, at least, nothing that matters. I never know what anyone is talking about. That's why I came here. I thought it would be a good place to start.' She smiled at Archie but he was not looking at her.

'I read a lot,' Archie said, still gazing across the bar.

'So do I', she agreed, 'but I never understand any of it.'

'Never?' Archie suddenly turned and looked at Isabel. She was shocked by his eyebrows. They moved wildly when he spoke, as though a sudden wind had come up from a corner of the room. 'I don't believe you never understand any of it, ever.'

'Well, that's how it feels,' Isabel looked at Archie who was now staring at her. She smiled brightly and then began to feel a little nervous, 'I think I preferred it when you weren't looking at me.'

Archie asked Isabel if he could get her another drink. Once they had finished those they went back to the university and sat through the afternoon of workshops together. Isabel watched the blackboard filling up with equations and formulae. Archie sat and stared straight ahead, occasionally taking notes. Isabel tried to see what he was writing but only managed once: Archie had written, in small neat letters, 'Buy Milk'.

On the following day they met again in the pub at lunchtime. Isabel was wearing a short, pink skirt that a lot of the male Marxists had spent the morning trying to look up. Archie did not try to look up Isabel's skirt, in fact, he did not seem to notice it. He either looked ahead in a studiously dreamy manner or stared right into Isabel's eyes. She found both habits equally unnerving, but after her confession about Marx, she trusted him. It would be a

crime not to have an affair after such openness Isabel
decided.

Three nights after the seminar, Isabel and Archie met to
go to the cinema. They went to see a Russian film made in
the 1930s. Before the film they talked.

'You go to the cinema often, do you?' Archie asked.

'Yes, I do. I find the cinema relaxing,' Isabel replied.

'Have you seen "Solaris" by Tarkovsky?' Archie asked.

'No,' replied Isabel.

'Neither have I.'

Isabel found the film she and Archie saw extremely
moving. During one bit mid-way through, she found
herself in tears. Archie sat perfectly expressionless, gazing
at the screen in front of him. Afterwards, when they had
walked to the underground and were about to leave on
separate lines, Archie put his arms around Isabel's waist.
He kissed her on the lips and said goodnight. When
Isabel stepped into the train she realised they hadn't
talked about the film they had just seen.

Four days later, Isabel rang up Archie and asked him to
come to a party at a big house where a friend of hers lived.
When he finally arrived at midnight with two bottles of
wine, he and Isabel sat in a dark corner discussing
Margaret Thatcher and books until about 3.00 a.m.

'Have you read *The History of Sexuality: Volume One* by
Michel Foucault?'

'No.'

'Neither have I.' Then Archie and Isabel kissed. They
danced for a while in between three and four o'clock.
Isabel did not introduce Archie to any of her friends.
Archie talked about himself. When he went to the toilet at
three thirty Isabel wanted to lie down on the dance floor,
she was so exhausted.

'Have you read the *Prison Notebooks* by Gramsci?'

'No.'

'Neither have I.'

Just before dawn, when the party began to wind down,

Archie said to Isabel, 'I'm getting tired. I think I'd better go home. I'll find a cab or something.' He paused and, without looking at her said, 'Would you like to come home with me?'

'OK,' said Isabel. 'It's not everyday I meet someone who'll admit to being as badly read as I am.' Archie did not reply.

When they got to Archie's flat and were sitting on the sofa drinking cups of tea he said, 'Well, I feel I've told you my life story.'

'Yes,' said Isabel, 'I guess you have.' She blushed, 'Part of it anyway.'

'You haven't told me much about yourself, Issy.'

'No.' Isabel smiled and then Archie kissed her on the mouth. He peeled off her clothes with his big hands and kissed her scar without asking where it had come from.

Maybe that's where it started, maybe that was where Isabel made the first mistake. Not talking about herself seemed to make her somehow less than herself. When she was with Archie both her personality and her past evaporated. They seemed to blow away like dry leaves, perhaps in the same wind that disturbed Archie's eyebrows. All she would confide was how much she did not know, and that very act seemed to have established in her an unbreakable silence.

Since Isabel felt she could not please Archie by regaling him with multifarious stories from her fascinating past lives she sought another way to attract his attention. The only way she could think of was that much dreaded way, through those infamous and self-denying constructs, feminine charms.

Isabel began to wear more make-up. She did her hair attractively, spending time on it. She wore short skirts and an array of clothes that were greeted with shouts from other men whenever she went out without Archie. One day when she was on her bicycle a man leaned out of his car window and said, 'I wish my face was your bicycle seat.' Isabel was left speechless as usual.

Archie didn't seem to notice the way Isabel looked, although occasionally she thought she could detect, somewhere in the depths of his stare, a kind of hunger. When they made love Isabel's body was filled not so much with desire, but with a longing to please. When he ran his big hand from her breast to her thigh it was not so much his touch that thrilled her, but the look on his face. She sometimes felt she would have given him almost anything.

Isabel began to grow faint, gradually becoming more and more transparent. At the end of each day the little strength she had left she devoted to seducing Archie and drawing him to her with his pleasure. Isabel thought that Archie was happy and that she probably seemed mysterious and beautiful to him. When he said, 'You are quiet Issy,' she knew it was not a question but a compliment.

At night, Isabel lay awake, watching Archie sleep. 'You don't know me at all,' she thought, but she didn't wake him up to point this out. That, too, was a mistake. During the day, from time to time, Isabel would catch Archie watching her from behind his great eyebrows but their only real form of communication was sex. They never ever read in bed.

The affair between Isabel and Archie continued for quite some time until one day, standing on an escalator, Isabel saw herself in a big mirror. As the moving staircase progressed upwards, she examined her reflection, staring into her own empty blue eyes. 'I am disappearing,' she said out loud. 'There's been a mistake. I've made a mistake.' The escalator carried her up and, once out on ground level, Isabel ran to the library. She took out a whole pile of books that she had never read, carried them all home and put them on to her bed.

Isabel spent that afternoon reading and in the evening

when Archie came home she said, 'Hello Archie. I've been reading.'

'You've been what, Isabel?'

'I said I've started to read again Archie. I went to the library today.'

'Issy,' he said, his eyebrows quivering slightly. 'Your lipstick is smudged.'

'What?' asked Isabel with surprise. Archie had made his first mistake. And nothing was the same ever again.

The Imperial War Museum

Before 1936 the Imperial War Museum was a mental asylum called Bethlem Royal Hospital. Many people were housed there, most of whom had been driven mad by the pressures of the Victorian era, and later, the First World War. In this large and imposing building women and men threw themselves against the barred windows and shivered without heat all winter long. Renfield himself probably lived there whilst being driven to distraction and a diet of flies by the nocturnal visits of Count Dracula. What could be a more fitting place to house a museum of war, an archive of the times when our individual madnesses become collective?

Despite the past of the building, the Imperial War Museum is a warm place to spend the afternoon for anyone with the slightest interest in war and propaganda. During opening hours it is populated by a handful of little boys and old men who wander from war to war admiring the guns and discussing the ammunition.

Carol had a passion for the Second World War. Some of her happiest childhood memories revolved around the evenings she and her father had spent watching documentaries about the war on television. She had sat on his knee and listened to him explain each battle in great detail, who had won, what the character of each

nation's army had been, and how many had died. Carol's
father had been a pilot during WW2. Some of his own
happiest memories revolved around flying planes during
the war that he always referred to as 'The War Against
Fascism'.

To Carol, who was born well over a decade after VE
Day, the Second World War represented a world very
different from her own, one that was completely contained by history books and films and graspable through
maps and statistics. The Second World War was, from her
abstracted and slightly odd perspective, a microcosm of
European history. It was a time of great tragedy, she
recognised that, but also a time of fascinating personalities and maze-like manoeuvres. For Carol, the war was
rather like one enormous board game made all the more
entertaining by its relationship to reality. She loved war
films, war novels, war poetry and war memorabilia;
everything about the Second World War intrigued her.

This passion was a secret. While other girls tortured
their mothers for new dolls, Carol and her father kept up
an enormous collection of toy soldiers. On rainy Sunday
afternoons they re-enacted battles on the floor of the
sitting-room. Carol's favourite was the invasion of the
Soviet Union by the Germans. She always made her father
the enemy, a role he undertook with great seriousness,
adopting the appropriate accent and goose-stepping into
the kitchen to fetch refreshments. He did not mind always
losing because it made him laugh to see his daughter so
excited as she brought in her Siberian troops on skis. 'I'll
get you now, Daddy, just you wait, YOU DON'T HAVE
WARM ENOUGH SHOES!' she would shout gleefully.
'Stupid Nazis, you forgot about the winter!' Her father's
little toy soldiers would begin to fall at an ever-increasing
pace until he would finally be forced to surrender to a
victorious Carol. 'I won,' she would say with pleasure.
'Thanks Daddy, thanks for the good war.'

The day after Carol left Fred she woke up in a heap of

bedclothes, feeling tear-stained and confused. She stretched out her legs and then winced with pain as she remembered what had happened. She and Fred would not be cooking breakfast together any longer. She got up, put on some clothes, and left her friend's flat, where she had spent the night, without really thinking.

The Imperial War Museum is set well back from the road, surrounded by a well-kept lawn. From the side, the building has narrow and tall windows that are set in the high forbidding walls of a mental hospital, but from the front it looks suitably grand. The footpath to the entrance is interrupted by a twin set of guns. These guns weigh approximately 100 tons each and sit heavily, pointing out towards Trafalgar Square and Westminster. They have a range of 18¼ miles which means that from their position at the entrance to the museum all of London could be devastated.

Still thinking about Fred, Carol walked up the footpath to the museum and, when she reached the guns, stopped underneath them. Looking up, she wondered, almost idly, where they had been active and at whom they might have been fired. On the ground was a plaque that said 'Do Not Climb On The Guns, You May Get Hurt'. Carol did not climb on the guns; instead she climbed the front stairs of the building and went inside the doors.

Once past the security check and the turnstile, Carol decided she would stroll through the museum without paying particular attention to any one war. It had been a long time since she had thought about the War. When Carol became a teenager she quickly discovered that boys found it odd that a nice girl like her should know so much about the Gothic Line. So she put her Allied Troops in boxes under the bed and began to collect lipstick and eye-shadow instead. The Cindy Doll that Carol had always said was a French resistance fighter she discarded along with other childhood toys.

Carol began to wander through the museum, letting all

the wars roll by her at once. Turning to the left, she entered World War One. She walked past a sign that said, 'The First World War and Its Origins' and then past a machine-gun with a burnt Union Jack draped over it and came to a stop in front of a model of a trooper of the 9th Lancers. He was sitting on a horse and looked a bit cramped inside the glass exhibition case. Despite this, the trooper had a particularly compassionate expression on his face, as if he were gazing out across history instead of at his own reflection in the glass. As Carol looked at him she thought that perhaps his expression had something to do with the battles he had seen. She stood and stared at the trooper on his solid, stuffed horse for several minutes until she noticed the sound of gunfire and marching, cannons booming in the distance, coming from another room deeper inside the museum.

The next room that Carol entered contained an exhibition about the Home Front. Back in the building's days as an asylum, this room had been used for women's ablutions. They had toiled over large steaming pots full of washing and, in the cold early morning light, had taken their monthly baths. The ablutions room was never particularly pleasant. It was dark like almost all the rooms in the building and constantly filled with steam. Bathing was not a quiet and contemplative activity in the asylum; the water, like the room, was either freezing or boiling. There was no privacy and as many as thirty women would have had to bathe at the same time.

The exhibit that the ablutions room now housed consisted mainly of a large group of female mannequins attired in a variety of uniforms that related to duties carried out in the homes, hospitals, kitchens, factories and all the other places where women worked during wartime. The mannequins were standing in groups of two or three with their heads bowed together, as if having a quiet chat whilst carrying on with their duties as wives and mothers to the troops. All were made of the same stiff mould, standing about five feet four inches tall with slight figures. Peering out from under their hats, their white plastic faces were blessed with quiet, calm expressions, like a row of identical Florence Nightingales.

Carol stared through the glass trying to work out what each one was doing. Signing documents, administering to the poor and sick, organising the Home Front: they were all acting with the same precise gestures and all had the same benevolent smile, frozen in perpetuity. Carol felt full of admiration for their fortitude. Then she noticed their hands. Whoever had ordered these ideal women had made some mistake; all the young female troops had the hands of male mannequins, big, gnarled and unwieldy, fit for battle and not for mothering at all.

Carol stood in front of this exhibition for a long time. One of the mock nurses reminded her of her grandmother. She stared at this mannequin who was poised to turn the page of a large official-looking register. In its blankness, the young woman's face was very serene, and the angle of her shoulders struck a chord in Carol's memory. But then, once again, the sound of gunfire drew Carol on, still deeper into the museum.

The next exhibition that caught Carol's attention was a room full of propaganda relating to the Spanish Civil War. Amongst the posters exhorting Britain to send food was a small collection of effects belonging to a young Oxford graduate who was killed in the early days of the war. Next to his membership card for the Young Communist League of Great Britain was a poem he had written to his girlfriend from the front. Carol read it and leaned against the glass cabinet thinking of Fred. He would never have written her poetry. With the young Communist's possessions there was also a small portrait of Lenin that he had carried with him into battle. Carol's first girlhood crush was on Lenin. She had a large portrait of him stuck up on her wall where other girls had David Cassidy. He, of course, hadn't had much to do with the Second World

War, but Carol didn't mind that at the time. He had made up for it in other ways.

Carol sighed and walked on, stopping to sit in front of a map of Europe. She traced the coast of Britain with her eyes and thought of her father in his plane, flying low over the Channel. He had said to her, time after time, while they lay together on the floor after gunning each other down, 'I never killed a man that I could see, sweetheart. Oh, I gunned down my share of German aeroplanes; that swastika made me see red. But, I never fought on the ground. No, I never shot a man I could see.' On hearing this Carol would nod sagely, believing she understood what he meant.

Next along there was a map of Britain and above it was a sign that read 'Britain and Its Role in the First World War'. Carol thought of her grandfather's brothers, killed in the trenches of the muddy Great War. All those great-uncles; she could picture them in the old sepia photographs her grandmother had shown her.

'Where are they now, Gran?' she would ask.

'Killed in the war,' her Gran would say. 'Shot up and gone to heaven.' Carol always had to struggle to stop herself asking an endless string of questions then, like 'How were they killed? Were they crushed by tanks or did a zeppelin, moving through the air like a very low, strange cloud, drop a bomb on them? Were they together, the brothers, did they cling to each other as they might have done when they were very small? Or did they die of dirty boredom as they crouched waiting in the trenches?'

An old man wandered over to where Carol was sitting. She could tell from the way he was looking at her that he was determined to talk about the war. 'Which war?' Carol wondered.

'Hello,' she said. 'Which war is your particular favourite?'

'Oh,' he said, 'well, I like World War Two the best, I think. It was my war. Bombs were bombs, guns were guns, planes were planes, and soldiers were soldiers. Not like today, nope. Take that Falklands War, over there in Room 23. Short, it was, a very short war. Sneaky too. Uh-huh,' he shook his head, 'don't care for these modern wars.' He gave a quiet snort and then seemed to fall asleep. Carol wandered into the next room. She could still hear the sound of gunfire, somewhere in the distance. She thought she could make out a German roar of greeting to the Führer.

Inside another glass cabinet stood a European soldier from the First World War, she wasn't sure from which country. He had camouflaging in his helmet and fake blood on the right arm of his uniform. Carol pushed her face up against the glass, smiling at the dummy. 'No one is going to hurt you here,' she whispered. 'The security guards wear uniforms but they aren't soldiers.' The mannequin did not reply. 'Where are you from?' she whispered, 'Ti amo, ich liebe dich, je t'adore.' When he didn't reply to that either, Carol turned away leaving behind a little steam patch on the glass.

Next she walked through rooms that had once been the large dining-hall of the asylum. Less than sixty years ago row upon row of hungry men and women sat on mean benches and were served a cruel gruel for their tea, laughed at by the orderlies who wore hats and long coats to protect themselves from the inmates. The men and women banged their metal cups on their metal plates like prisoners anywhere.

Carol's father had been taken prisoner, briefly at the end of the war. 'Oh they were horrible, those Germans, Carol. Horrible. That camp, it was a nasty place. And when we found out what they'd been doing to all those Jewish people, and the poofters, and the Communists, why it was enough to make you want to fight the war single-handed. I don't know, lovey, people are mad, they really are. I often think to myself that it's the politicians who are the real nutters, all the daft things they say and do. You'll be a lucky woman if these games are the closest you ever get to a real war, Carol. But, in the meantime, I've just taken that whole regiment over there prisoner. Surrender or die!'

The dining-room now housed a collection of vehicles: two Spitfire aeroplanes, rather like the one her father had flown, were suspended above a pair of rolling guns, a tank, several extremely heavily armoured vehicles, a model torpedo, an Italian submarine called 'The Human Torpedo' that looks like a canoe built to travel underwater with its operators wearing diving gear, and the 'Biber', the smallest submarine in the German army. Built in 1944, it could carry one soldier and two torpedoes. These machines which were made to endure war had ended up as exhibits in a museum. Carol climbed up on to the tiny submarine. Beneath the hatch was a crouch space with windows all around it. Carol pulled the lid down on top of her. The metal of the submarine was cold and smelled just like the metal frame of a set of swings Carol had played on as a child, a smell remarkably like that of blood. Several little boys stared as Carol sat listening. From her position inside the submarine, the recordings of cannon-fire and submachine-gun drill that resounded throughout the museum sounded like the massed cries of human voices. Carol was sure she could hear the repetitive, lonely wails of the mad, locked away without family or friends or anything to add comfort to their own individual wars against reality.

The Whole Story

They scurried away from the scene of their crime like rats, horrible, heartless, and terrifyingly insidious. They went off together in the borrowed Porsche, with the money they had been lent and the time they had stolen. She, Louise, was devastated. She shouted after them as they drove off, 'You rats! How could you?' then stomped back into the house with torrents of abuse streaming through her mind. How could they? It was easy. They had lost their human hearts a long time ago and given themselves over to absolute vileness.

That was what Louise thought but the Whole Story went more like this:

Mary and Joseph were given a rare opportunity for a vacation. Mary thought that this might upset Louise, but she quickly decided that it would be stupid to let such a good idea go by. Joseph simply didn't have to think about it at all. It just seemed like such a good idea.

And really, on the outside, it was a good idea, like putting one and one together and getting two, except that in this case that meant leaving a third one out. Joseph and Mary were not having an affair. Somehow if they had been it would have been easier for Louise. She could have been completely dramatic and said, 'Get out of my life and don't come back, you loathsome twosome. You've

37

broken my heart.' But neither they, nor Louise and Joseph, nor Louise and Mary were having affairs. The dawn of the New Puritanism is upon us.

Louise felt broken-hearted and isolated, even before they'd gone away. She couldn't sleep at night and took drugs to calm herself down, but no chemicals worked. She longed to be heavily sedated. She felt her emotions were like a mad rhinoceros rampaging through her head. She longed to be put down.

Poor Louise. She's really got it all wrong. She keeps trotting out all the wrong emotions on all the wrong occasions. Some people are like that, conscientious objectors to the Plain Truth. You're over the top Louise. You've got to see the whole story. Face it.

'Why didn't you think of me in all of your planning?' Louise had shouted at Mary before she and Joseph had left. 'How could you not consider how I feel about you two going off together like newlyweds? How could you do something that hurts me so?'

'But Louise,' Mary had protested, 'that's not the Whole Story. You've got to look at the whole story. I just don't see it your way.' And yet, Louise could not see any story other than her own. She tried, and failed.

Joseph and Mary were having a lovely time. They drove through village after village, stopping for tea or alcohol wherever and whenever they wished. Joseph and Mary worked very hard at their respective careers, devoting huge amounts of time to what they passionately believed in. Like most dedicated people they weren't thanked nearly often enough and this little holiday was their way of thanking themselves. 'I deserve this,' they both thought as they whizzed by towns and fields. 'This is just what I needed. What a good idea! Imagine borrowing a Porsche and just taking off, as if nothing else mattered. How wonderful. How satisfying. How fun!'

Fun was important to both Joseph and Mary. Mary especially: she felt like she had had several non-fun years in a row and that her time was long overdue. Joseph liked fun as well, in its place. He wasn't one for complete, unbridled fun-all-the-time. Joseph needed his dose of hard work and painful ideological deliberation to really enjoy himself.

Louise, however, felt she had forgotten how to have fun. She kept this a secret from all but her most cherished friends. Everyone else thought Louise was clever and carefree. She was fairly successful at her job and had a certain amount of what appeared to be fun. And occasionally it was actual fun for Louise. That was before Joseph and Mary drove off and left her behind in a big salty puddle of tears. They sped down the M1 at 100 miles an hour, singing along to pop songs on the radio and smiling at the slower, more boring cars which they passed. Long after they'd gone Louise was still shouting, 'You rats! And Porsches are ideologically unsound too!' But they didn't hear her.

'Tra-la-la-la-la,' they sang. 'A holiday.'

'Gosh, Mary,' said Joseph, 'look at those lambs over there. Aren't they lovely.'

'Oh yes, oh, aren't they sweet!' squealed Mary. 'Isn't spring wonderful,' she sighed, thinking of all the flowers and blossoming trees they weren't seeing from their Porsche on the M1. This was probably the closest she and Joseph came to falling in love.

But Louise could not imagine that all Joseph and Mary were doing on this holiday was speeding in the Porsche and mooning over lambs. She was being driven wild with animalistic jealousy.

Louise decided it was time for action. She divided all her possessions in half. This took rather a long time because although Louise didn't own much, she had to cut or tear all the clothes, saw the table and chair and chest, use a glass-cutter on the mirror, take an axe to the cassette-player, and rip all the books. It was a slow and arduous task. Louise was rather lucky that Joseph and

Mary had gone off for a fortnight. In a way, she was stealing back their borrowed time.

Once she had divided everything, except of course the clothes she was wearing, Louise put one half in Joseph's room, and the other in Mary's. They both had big rooms so this wasn't too difficult, although it did make rather a mess. Louise had a few problems deciding which half of what should go to whom, but she quickly made a general rule that the left-hand side should go to Joseph, the right-hand to Mary, and stuck to that except in places where it was obviously the other way around.

When she had finished she sat in the kitchen and felt calm and satisfied for a moment, but then she began thinking about Joseph and Mary, attempting to imagine what they could possibly be doing. She thought they might be parked by the sea somewhere, sipping champagne and wearing white linen suits that matched the Porsche. Or perhaps they were sipping champagne in an enormous bed in a posh hotel with a line of Porsches parked outside, the balcony windows opening on to the sea. Or maybe they were sipping champagne and making love in a field of frangipani with the Porsche grazing quietly next to them. Louise thought that Joseph and Mary could be up to almost anything.

Louise sat in the kitchen coming up with scenario after scenario, each one more decadent than the last, each one making her a bit more miserable. If either Joseph or Mary had known what Louise was thinking they would have said, 'Oh Louise, how ridiculous. We just thought it seemed like a good idea. We heard Opportunity knock so we answered the door and said, "Yes, we'll take it." We didn't think of you. Why should we?'

But Louise couldn't face it, and she couldn't face Joseph and Mary returning from their holiday, all relaxed and sleek, like the Porsche they had borrowed. She felt she'd tried everything. So, she did the only thing left for her to do, aside from ending it all.

Louise stole a Porsche, took the ferry to France, and became a successful painter. Perhaps her greatest work is an abstract picture, dark brooding blocks of colour with blood-red slashes across them, entitled 'The Rhinoceros Vindicates Jealousy'.

In Montreal

In Montreal Christine was foreign for the first time. She had never been outside the enormous and empty western province in which she had grown up. In fact, she had hardly been away from the small, mountain town where her family lived. To Christine, Montreal seemed as romantic and distant as Paris. Ever since she was a small girl and had seen Quebec on the television, watched those gritty politicians with their gravelly voices and thick accents, she had wanted to go and live there. So, when she was seventeen she packed her bags and, with the money she had made car-hopping in the summer at the Drive-In Restaurant, she boarded an aeroplane and began her adult life.

In Montreal Christine could not speak the language. When she arrived in the terminal and asked for directions to the city in her high school French, she knew immediately that she was out of her depth. The woman at the information desk replied to her in English. But that did not stop Christine. She was brave, determined and stubborn, as only seventeen-year-old girls can be.

Christine knew exactly what she was going to do with her new life in Montreal. She had told her parents she was going to get a job, save some money and then go to university, but she had no intention of doing anything as

mundane as that. Christine was going to speak French,
dress in black, smoke Gauloises, live by herself, and, best
of all, become a lapsed Catholic. In the small town where
she had grown up most people were either Presbyterians
or members of the United Church, a distinctly Canadian
mixture of protestant religions that resembled a sort of
extremely low Anglican. Christine was bored with that
now. She wanted a religion with some dignity and
mystery so that when she rejected it, as she knew she
would, she'd have the pleasure of rejecting something
particularly rich.

Within a week of her arrival Christine had a job wiping
tables and clearing dishes in a café in the bottom of Les
Terraces, a shopping complex on St Catherine Street in
downtown Montreal. It was one of those totally plastic
little places that Montreal enterprise is so bad at, a
sub-American kind of dive, decorated in orange and
lime-green with mushroom-like tables sprouting out of
the concrete floor and dingy mirrors on the walls. Les
Terraces, like much of downtown Montreal, is indoors
and underground. At Le Hamburger the ventilation
worked against the heating and the result was a very hot
hamburger bar with grease hanging in the air. But, to
Christine, the most extraordinary thing about Le Hamburger was that, despite all appearances, everything about it was absolutely Québécois. 'Un hamburger, s'il
vous plaît.'

Along with the job, which paid much less than the legal
minimum wage, a fact she didn't have enough French to
complain about, Christine found somewhere to live. From
an advert in the window of a small corner tabac she rented
a one-room apartment at the top of four flights of stairs
down by the river in East Montreal. The windows were
cracked and the small radiator hissed and sighed while it
pumped out heat. The hot-plate in the corner was coated
with grime, and the mattress was lumpy. The obligatory
bare lightbulb hung from the ceiling in the middle

of the room. Christine loved it, of course. It was all hers.

Montreal was all hers as well – Christine felt this as she strolled along the city's streets. The churches, the parks, the cafés, the bar-restaurants that stay open all night, even the taverns on the corners that still did not allow women through their doors; in those first months she often felt like embracing it all. But Montreal was much slower to accept Christine. More often than not when she greeted its inhabitants with her very bad but enthusiastic French she would be answered in English or not at all. The Canadian Language War was at its height and Christine frequently became an unwitting casualty of the hostilities. But youth, determination, and zeal protected her as she calmly got on with her life.

During the daytime, from 7.00 a.m. to 5.00 p.m., Christine cleaned up after the boys who hung out at Le Hamburger. While they dealt acid and punched each other on the forearms, she picked up coffee cups and wiped ketchup off the tables. She listened to their raucous conversation, catching the odd word in English: 'car', 'bar', 'pizza', 'acid', and 'hashish'.

From the big bookstore further down St Catherine Street Christine bought herself a book called *How to Speak French* and in the evenings once home from work she read it diligently, practising out loud in front of the mirror. 'Bonjour, madame. Bonjour, mademoiselle. Comment ça va?' she'd say to herself. 'Ça va bien, et vous? Voulez-vous un hamburger? Non, merci. Je suis fatiguée.'

On Sundays, her one day away from Le Hamburger, Christine went to mass. She was making a tour of all the Catholic churches in Montreal. This project would take her years to complete, but Christine was undaunted by this in the same way that she was undaunted by much about her new life. She started off with the big ones and on her first Catholic Sunday went to Notre-Dame in Vieux Montreal. Its old world splendour pleased her; the stained glass and high arched ceilings made her feel something she imagined might be akin to Faith.

On the second Sunday Christine attended mass in St Joseph's Oratory, one of the biggest Catholic churches in North America. It sits up on the north-east side of Mont Royale, together with the huge, electrically-lit cross that stands further up the mountain. Christine climbed the hundreds of steps that lead up to the church, steps she would later learn to her blatantly protestant distaste that thousands of pilgrims had climbed, and were still climbing, on their knees every year. Inside the Oratory, Christine was impressed by the grandeur of the building and the extreme religiosity of the ceremony. She lit a candle and then fell asleep during the service. The mystery of Catholicism was a complete enigma to Christine and besides, it was all in French.

Back at Le Hamburger on Monday morning, Christine communicated with her boss, a small and dark Québécois man named Rene, by smiling, nodding and then going back to work without the slightest idea what he had been saying. He, however, seemed pleased enough with her and Christine believed that he must not realise she could not speak French but merely thought she was a bit quiet. When the boys who hung out directed their conversation towards her, she merely smiled and occasionally said 'Oui'. She had learned by that time how to say 'Oui' with the appropriate Montreal accent rendering it completely unlike anything she had learned in high school. The boys were not convinced.

As spring gradually moved into summer the over-heating at Les Terraces became over-air-conditioning. Christine continued to work at the hamburger bar and incorporated into her Sunday tour of the churches lengthy diversions into the Parc Mont Royale where she would spend the afternoon lying in the sun reading French grammar books. She was progressing well with the language, warming up to it with the weather. By June she had learned enough to ask for more money from her boss at Le Hamburger.

One day, a boy who hung out, leaning his thin frame against the orange plastic table for most of the afternoon, drinking cups of Rene's foul coffee and, occasionally, dribbling ketchup over the limp fries that were the speciality of the place, looked up at Christine while she was wiping away spilt sugar from the next table.

'Hello,' he said, in strongly accented English. 'Where are you from?'

'Quoi?' replied Christine.

'Come on,' he said, 'I know you are not French. I know you are an Anglo. Speak up, eh? Where are you from?'

Christine smiled at him. 'Mais, je suis Français.'

The boy laughed and said, 'You are about as French as Rene's hamburgers.' Christine continued to wipe tables while all around her the boys, No. 7s dangling from their mouths, laughed.

By August, the hottest and stickiest month in Montreal, Christine was reading novels in French and beginning to build up a small collection of books in her room. She was reading Colette and Marie-Claire Blais and had even embarked upon À la recherche du temps perdu. During the evening, after she finished work, Christine would leave the cold underground environment of Les Terraces and walk down St Catherine Street, heading east. When she reached St Denis she would turn to the right and find a seat in one of the many cafés that spill out onto the sidewalk. There she would sit sipping a beer and read, ignoring the sweat that ran in rivulets down her back. Usually some jazz would be wafting out of the café and Christine would feel, as the verbs, nouns and adjectives came off the page and told her stories, that she was beginning to understand her adopted language. She would sit and read Proust very happily for several hours until she felt her eyes grow heavy, then, just as the cafés were beginning to fill up with Montrealers out for the evening, she would pick up her book, empty her glass of beer, and walk home to her little room.

At about ten o'clock one evening, the time Christine usually headed off, a young woman with dark eyes and a mass of curly hair stopped beside her table. 'Bonjour,' she said, and still speaking in French, 'Is anyone sitting here?'

'No,' said Christine, in French, 'please sit down. I was just about to leave.'

'Oh,' said the woman, 'you are not French?'

'No,' said Christine, 'I come from the West.'

'But you speak French? Where do you live, here, in Montreal?'

'Yes, I live down by the river.'

'By yourself?'

'Yes.'

'But that is very brave,' replied the woman, who then introduced herself. Marie-Sylvie was a student at the university nearby. She came from a small town up the St Lawrence River and did not speak one word of English. Christine talked to her in French without pausing to think as she did so. They ordered several beers together and watched while the activity on St Denis grew more frenetic as the night drew on.

'So,' said Marie-Sylvie. 'You live all by yourself in a tiny room by the river and you work every day in a greasy café wiping up after obnoxious boys who treat you badly. You are paid very little. On Sundays you go to church, although you are not Catholic and the rest of the time you spend reading French grammar books. Why?'

'Well,' replied Christine in her young and steady voice. 'It seemed the only way to begin to learn how to think in French.'

Around midnight Christine got up to leave. It was still very hot and when she stood she suddenly felt quite drunk.

'Au revoir. Will we meet again?' she asked Marie-Sylvie whose dark hair was damp with sweat.

'Au revoir,' said Marie-Sylvie, 'I come here often; I am sure we will.'

Christine wove her way through the tables of the café and began to walk back down St Denis towards St Catherine Street.

The Self-Loathing Diet
or How To Hate Yourself
Into Thin Air

There were days when Sophia Gaynor thought of herself as fat and there were days when she thought of herself as thin. These two states of mind bore no relation to her actual weight. Sometimes the fat days stretched into weeks, months and even longer (her entire adolescence). But the days when she felt thin were less frequent and rarely lasted much beyond a week.

On her thin days Sophie was like a butterfly flitting among tropical plants, light, colourful, and delicate. Sometimes she was like the tropical flower itself, flamboyant, bright, heady. On those good thin days she would have all the self-confidence in the world; she would feel she could conquer anything. She felt, in a word, womanly.

On her fat days Sophie was more like a harpie than a butterfly, swooping through the air screaming at herself with rage. Or she would be quiet like an over-ripe tropical fruit, soft, smelly, fermenting. She would hide herself in voluminous clothes and say no to most social arrangements. She'd go into work with a long face and when people asked how she was she'd imagine what they'd really wanted to say was, 'Christ, you've gained weight Sophie! What have you been up to, sublimating your sorrows?' No one, of course, ever said that but Sophie thought they might all the same.

Most of her female friends were secret weight-watchers and dieters. In public they'd talk about how they'd given up dieting years ago and were now just happy to be the way they were, but Sophie knew that their refrigerators were bulging with low fat cottage cheese and calorie-free breakfast supplements. She'd been shopping for clothes with them, she knew what they thought when they looked at themselves in the mirror.

'Oh my God,' Sophie would say, 'am I that ugly? This dress / skirt / bathing suit / cocktail dress makes me look about twenty pounds overweight.' She'd turn around and look at herself from behind. 'Oh my God, look at that. Thank Christ I don't ever have to walk behind myself.' And her friends would respond in a similar vein. They swore a lot when they went shopping and then, on their own, they'd swear to themselves to slim, just like Sophie.

But dieting had never been one of Sophie's greatest talents.

'Self denial,' as her friend Louise had once said, 'is what being a woman is all about.' At the time Sophie had thought Louise was referring simply to food.

Self-denial is a difficult commandment to live life abiding. One must deny oneself pastries and ice-cream, second helpings and snacks. But as well as the extras, slimming requires abstinence from more basic items, like butter and jam on toast in the morning, omelettes and chips for lunch, avocados and alcohol at supper, and that's what makes self-denial painful and anti-social.

Sophie was not very good at saying no. In fact it usually wouldn't occur to her until after the offending item of food was slipping down her gullet. She'd think to herself, 'If I hadn't buttered that I would have saved fifty calories . . . if I hadn't drunk that I wouldn't look like I do.' That line of thought inevitably led to darker pastures, the spooky nighttime fields on the bleaker side of dieting. Somehow, on fat days, Sophie always ended up treading that lonely path, dragging herself along by the spare tyre to the big sign on the side of the hill that reads, YOU ARE FAT. When she reached this point she would get down on her knees and blubber incoherently, 'I shouldn't have eaten it, I should do more leg-lifts, I should swim five times a week, I should cut out breakfast completely, I should get a night-job as well so I don't have time to eat, I should get my jaw wired shut, I should take a big pair of shearing scissors and cut all this extra bulk away, I should sell my refrigerator, I should fast for a week, I should take diet pills and laxatives and speed, I should buy all my clothes two sizes too small and not give in until I can wear them.'

Sophie knew that all her friends went through this on their fat days. She knew that they too walked the Self-Loathing Trail up the big hill and worried about their hips and their thighs and how a carpenter's level would behave on their stomachs. But they never said a word about it, never even hinted at it, because they all knew where that would lead: long, rainy nights in the kitchen, sitting around drinking beer, eating potato crisps and moaning about how fat they all felt. That did not appeal to Sophie. She did not want to share her self-contempt.

Still, Sophie's sanity and self-image were saved by her thin days. She would get up early and have a bath, her body feeling absolved and light, free of the fat day's stockpile of toxins and waste. She'd run to work on air and fly through her day, flirting with everyone and not minding the construction workers when they shouted at her. Her clothes would feel loose, colourful, sexy, and in the evening she'd feel relaxed and fulfilled and optimistic.

On one of those days Sophie was in the pub with her friends when Louise said, 'Sophie you look great today, have you lost some weight?'

'No, I don't worry about dieting any more,' Sophie replied, 'I gave up on that years ago. It's the tyranny of the women's magazines that forces that on us.'

'Yes,' her friend nodded and agreed, 'I could swear my boyfriend reads those things. He knows more about cellulite than I do.'

'Cellulite?' thought Sophie feeling lightning-struck. 'Cellulite. Maybe that's my problem. I'd never looked at it that way.' Sophie was silent. It was as if Louise had spotted her pretending to be a butterfly and put a net over her head.

At home that night, Sophie pulled out one of her glossy women's magazines, full of advice about how to improve appearances. Page twenty told her about how terrible it is when boyfriends put pressure on their girlfriends to change and how girlfriends shouldn't put up with it, and page twenty-one told her about how to change so that men will find you more attractive. Sophie turned to the section on cellulite. 'You know you've got cellulite,' said the magazine, 'when you grab hold of your thigh and squeeze it and the skin dimples and puckers like bread dough full of air bubbles.' Sophie grabbed hold of her thigh and squeezed it as hard as she could. Her skin dimpled and puckered like bread dough absolutely riddled with air bubbles. She felt herself go pale. She felt faint. Then she let go of her thigh and lay back down on her bed.

'I've got cellulite,' she said out loud. 'Oh my God. What do I do now?' She grabbed hold of the women's magazine and squeezed it then reopened it to the page she'd been reading.

'The only way to get rid of this unsightly mess', the magazine read, 'is through rigorous exercise, massage and avoiding all foods that are known to aid fat retention.' Sophie's young and strong heart sank down to her ankles. 'Start your new regime today.

'Part One: Establish a regular routine of leg-lifts, thigh-rolls, splits, twists, ballet turns, and other thigh-stretching exercises. Swim as frequently as possible.

'Part Two: Go down to the chemist and buy a Betsy Dorreen All-Over Skin Treatment Kit. Be sure to get the one with Massage Conditioner No. 10 in it. Use this after your daily bath. At least ten minutes every night should be spent on thigh massage.

'Part Three: Go on a diet. Do not eat anything with fat in it, including food cooked in oil and oil-based salad dressings. Avoid sugar, dairy products, meat, and all heavy food.

'You should see results within a fortnight.'

Sophie put the magazine down. She wondered if any-one had noticed she had cellulite. As no one had squeezed her thighs lately it seemed unlikely unless she had had it for years without being aware of it. Once again she grabbed her thigh and examined the puckers and dim-ples. The sight of it made her feel ill. Bodies can be so disgusting. It's horrible to think what people have under their clothes.

So, the new regime began for Sophie the very next day. She skipped breakfast and went to the chemist's on her way to work. At the office she cried off from a previously arranged social engagement and went straight home at six o'clock to start on the exercises. She felt exhausted after the first ten leg-lifts but that didn't stop her, she kept on going right through the recommended routine. Then she bathed and tried out the new products.

The massage kit came with an assortment of lotions and poultices but the most interesting thing in it was the massage device itself. It was shaped like a big, fat, wide banana with a movable handle attached to it. One side was very rough, the other side was covered in large bumps. The instructions said that it had two functions, one, to get rid of old skin – that was the rough side – and another, to massage and, thus break-up, the cellulite. Sophie read all this carefully then she applied the

appropriate lotions and poultices and rubbed and mas-
saged until her thighs were very pink. Then she went to
bed with a well-known diet book called *Ten Days to
Renewed Self-Confidence and Glamour*. The first line said,
'So, you think you're fat and you've decided to do
something about it. Well, you've come to the right place.'
Sophie began to read, thanking her lucky stars all the
while for not having forced her to live in a beach culture
where she might have had to expose her thighs daily.

Sophie adhered to her new regime very successfully,
but during those days of self-denial and hard work, she
did not feel very happy, nor did she have a single thin
day. Her butterfly clothes wilted in the closet like tropical
flowers laid waste by a storm. Even when she began to
notice a difference in her thighs, which were constantly
bright pink and becoming very hard, her spirits did not
improve. Very simply, she felt fat. Fat, fat, fat. Like a
beached whale, a giant in a tiny land. No room at the Inn.

The regime finished and Sophie had cellulite-free
thighs. To celebrate she went out and bought a mini-skirt
which she wore to a party the next weekend where she
drank rather a lot of beer, the more fattening of alcholic
drinks, and ate potato crisps without giving her diet a
second thought. Feeling miserable despite the length of
her brightly coloured skirt, she stood by herself and made
no effort to talk to anyone. Her friends avoided her when
they saw the dark clouds in her eyes. She guzzled beer
like a petrol-starved Cadillac and crushed the potato
crisps between her teeth like a steam-roller on glass.
Under her breath she repeated, 'I'm having a good time;
I have great thighs.'

Later in the evening when the storm clouds in her eyes
had lifted to a dense fog, a stranger stumbled up to her.
She watched as he stood in front of her swaying on his
unsteady legs.

'Great skirt,' he said smiling. 'Great thighs.' Sophie
looked on, while, as though in slow-motion replay, the

man bent over and grabbed her right leg with both hands. She hardly felt his fingers as they sank into her flesh and stood absolutely still while he squeezed her thigh. Fascinated and totally abstracted, as if she was watching someone else, she stared as he pinched her leg and slowly bent even lower to kiss her. He looked up from just below her hemline and, still smiling, said, 'You're like a peach, sweet and firm. I could bite you and eat you right here.'

Sophie started as if waking from a dream. She reached down and grabbed the man by the hair, pulling him up to his full height which was much greater than her own. Then with her free hand she slapped him across the face using as much force as she could muster. As he howled she realised that perhaps cellulite wasn't her only enemy after all.

Tiny Lies

Occasionally there is a story told about someone who has disappeared without trace. After a long search, friends and relatives eventually give the missing person up for dead. They resume their lives, recover from their grief, and may even make a grave on which to leave flowers. Then one day an acquaintance who knew the missing person vaguely and is on a vacation in a distant part of the country reports a sighting. Late at night, in a bar, they meet an apparent stranger who, after a long conversation, they realise must be that missing person from all those years ago. They want to ask, 'Why did you do it? What happened?' but they also want to avoid embarrassment so dare not, just in case they are mistaken.

And so it transpires that the missing person may not be dead. Once again, there is doubt. They could have simply left their proverbial clothes on the beach and gone down to Liverpool or London, taken on a new identity and embarked on a completely new life, perhaps changing their appearance and even the way they speak, blow their nose, or laugh. They might have forgotten their previous life, blanked it. They don't want to be found out. And, back at home, the friends and family listen to the description of the holiday encounter and wonder if it could possibly be true. All they can think to ask is 'Why?'

Unusual perhaps, but this happens often enough to be part of that subterranean cave full of stories our culture digs up from time to time. More frequently people make a kind of partial break by remaining where they are but ceasing to ring up old friends. They leave the job they did everyday for ten years and start a new one, or become unemployed and lose touch. They move to a new city and tell tiny lies about their previous existence. They break off with a lover and stop being part of the social circle in which the lover moves. They fall out with their family and decide to cut the ties in a final, dramatic kind of way. They change continents, or maybe they just dye their hair. They run away from something they don't like and, in the process, believe that they've recreated themselves.

After Monica had the abortion, the relationship she was in shattered. Somehow there was too much guilt and pain for it to continue. She and Chris attempted to keep it going; after all they did feel bonded together in some strange way, if only in their mutual loss. But Monica was angry and that did not help. She felt she had suffered and that Chris had refused to acknowledge it; he'd been too wrapped up in his own difficulties. They sliced each other up with long and sharp arguments until, finally, their relationship lay in pieces around their feet. It was almost a relief, but not quite.

Monica decided to walk away. She packed her bags and divided up all the possessions which had made their home. She took the teapot and left him the percolator. He was happy with that never having enjoyed their domesticity anyway. Rolling up her poster, she looked at him and said, 'Well Chris, I hope you're satisfied. Shame about the messy bits though. I have to say, I feel well fucked over.'

'Oh you do, do you Monica? Well, I have to say that I feel a bit fucked over as well. And that poster is mine.'

She considered moving in with one of her friends, but knew that none of them really wanted that despite their offers. Monica had this idea that everybody disapproved of her after the abortion. They weren't anti-choice, Monica's friends, they were simply uncomfortable with Monica's fuck-up, Monica's pain, Monica's depression, Monica's deteriorating relationship, and the way when they all got drunk on Friday night Monica would always end up in floods of tears babbling about her mother's dreams.

'What do you mean, Monica, when you say your mother's heart would break if she knew what you'd done? Your mother hasn't got anything to do with your relationship with Chris. She is not an invisible force passing judgment on your every action.'

'Oh yes she is,' Monica would reply. 'If she knew what I've done . . . she doesn't even think pre-marital kissing is a good idea, let alone pre-marital sex. Oh my God, what if she was right and I am wrong? She always says it's the woman who is left to suffer. She always says that.'

'Oh yeah? And I bet she also says that sex is a marital duty, doesn't she? Lie back and think of the Falkland Islands?' Monica felt misunderstood. Maybe she was, maybe she wasn't. But she was definitely unhappy and she needed a change.

So Monica decided that she would attempt to make a fresh start. This idea grew bigger and the restart became a clean break, and the clean break became a move, and the move progressed from around the corner to a different town and before she knew what had happened, Monica found herself in London with a new job, a flat, a routine to her week and a new attitude to life. She left Chris and her girlfriends behind and there seemed no point in telling them where she was going.

At the new job when people asked what Monica had done before she gave an elaborately edited account revealing only those bits that were relevant to her new position. When the woman at the next desk asked why she had left her home town, Monica told her that she'd wanted a change. Then when the man at another desk asked her, in a predatory kind of way, if she had a boyfriend, she'd panicked and said that she was married. And when her boss, upon discovering that she was married, asked her if she had any children, Monica winced and shook her head. Hearing the other women sitting around at lunch telling each other their medical tales of woe, Monica refrained from discussing her own. She didn't want to tell anybody anything.

Yet, when Monica went home at night and looked in the mirror she saw herself, her same old self, the face she had grown up with. Same old body, same old scars. So the next move was cosmetic. Monica went to the local hair-dressing school and bought a completely new hairstyle. She gave the student free rein and he transformed the straight blondish hair that Chris had run his hands through, the same hair that had gone lanky and dull while she was in the hospital, into a short auburn bob. Then she acquired a new wardrobe. She took up cigarettes and lost weight. Lying in the bath late one night she decided to paint her toenails red. She sold all her jewellery, the tiny stones she wore in her ears, the gold bracelets, the locket which had been given to her by Chris, and bought some big silver hoop earrings and large clunky bracelets. She took to wearing scent. Monica spent her evenings in the big city that she didn't know at all plotting her trans-formation.

One of the other women at work who sat opposite her and watched these rapid changes was intrigued. 'You get better looking everyday, Monica sweetheart,' she said to her one day. 'I'm having a party on Friday night. Would you like to come?' Siobhan had followed Monica into the women's toilets. 'There won't be any people from the office there. Here's an invite. It's got my address on it. Come about ten. Oh yeah,' she said, smiling, 'bring your husband.'

'Oh,' said Monica, blushing, 'he doesn't like parties

very much ... but I'd like to come.' As Siobhan walked toward the door Monica called out, 'Thanks.'

That Friday at lunchtime, Monica went down to the shops and bought a party outfit: a little black dress and some new tights. At five o'clock she rushed home and took a long bath, this time painting her fingernails as well as her toenails. She spent a long time powdering her body and stepping on and off the scales. Drinking beer as she worked, she put on her make-up and then, just before it was time to go, she slipped on the new dress and the black patterned tights. Her mother had always told her not to wear black as it is the colour for mourning. 'Well,' thought Monica, 'I am in mourning. I'm mourning all that time I wasted with Chris. All that spent passion.'

Monica took a cab to the party and, reaching Siobhan's house well before ten, went into the pub on the corner. She drank more beer sitting by herself at a small table. The place was fairly empty and nobody gave her a second look. As Monica sat, she inspected her outfit.

'I'm twenty-five years old. I'm married, no, I'm separated. I've got red hair and I smell of a sort of musky perfume. I smoke long cigarettes and ... I come from France and my name is really Monique ... no, no.' Monica sipped her beer and smiled to herself. After a while, she picked up her handbag and walked over to the party.

Siobhan lived in a medium-sized, two-bedroom flat with her best friend Diane. They had worked hard to prepare for the party, all kinds of snacks and a punch were set out on a big table in the kitchen. The sitting-room had been cleared out to make room for dancing and the coats went into Siobhan's bedroom, while in Diane's room big cushions were scattered on the floor where people could sit and talk. When Monica walked in there were only about fifteen people there but the hostesses were already fairly drunk. Siobhan got Monica a drink and introduced her to Diane who wanted to know where she had found her dress, a question that pleased Monica immensely. They chatted for a while about shops and clothes, then more people came in and Monica was jostled into the kitchen. Standing beside the refrigerator, she downed a couple of glasses of punch when she thought no one was looking and helped herself to some food. Siobhan kept coming in and out of the kitchen introducing everyone in sight and giggling, nervously. Monica smiled at her calmly. She drank the punch at a steady speed and began to feel quite comfortable. When Siobhan introduced her again to Diane she felt ready for conversation.

'So Diane, where do you work?'

'Oh,' replied Diane, 'at a similar sort of place to you. Boring, dead boring. Don't like it much, I want to do something more interesting. Do you like your job?'

'Uh,' said Monica, hesitating, 'no, well, I mean, uh, no.' In fact, Monica did enjoy her work but it didn't seem appropriate to say so. Everything was still new and exciting to her.

'All I really like about my job is the holidays. Siobhan and I are going to Spain next month. Have you ever been there?'

'Uh,' said Monica hesitating again, 'yes. Yes, I've been to Spain.' She hadn't.

'Oh yeah? Did you like it, was it nice?'

'Yes . . . good food. Lots of sun. Cheap. I went with my husband before we were married. We're separated now.' Monica said, laughing, 'I guess we didn't have enough holidays together!'

'Oh, I know just what you mean,' Diane said in a sympathetic tone. 'You need lots of time to relax together for a relationship to survive these days. My boyfriend and I broke up late last year and I think it's because we never had more than a Sunday morning together for relaxation. I tried to get us away on a holiday, but he didn't even have time for a weekend off. That's what happens when you live in London; it's so hard to get out of it.' Diane paused and downed another glass of punch. 'And then, of course I got pregnant. That didn't help things either.'

'You got pregnant,' Monica said, paling.

'Yes, yes. It was stupid I know, but we all make mistakes. We used to get drunk and forget to use the stuff. You must know what it's like, don't you?' she said, looking at Monica rather helplessly.

'Did you have the child?' Monica asked, barely audible above the general roar of the party.

'Are you kidding? Me, have a baby? I couldn't, I didn't even consider it. We didn't even get on that well. He would have been a lousy father and I would have been a worse mother.'

'Oh,' said Monica, staring into her punch. 'I'm sorry.'

'What's there to be sorry about? Worse things can happen. I'm resilient, or so Siobhan tells me. You're tough, old girl, that's what she says to me. Tough I say, but not that tough. Oh, there's Barry, I'd better go and say hello. See you in a bit Monica.' Diane smiled confidently and walked off towards a good-looking man who had just appeared in the kitchen.

Monica leaned heavily on the fridge. Thinking about the space between her legs, the part of her body that had burned with such pain so recently, she remembered with terrible clarity how it had felt to be overwhelmed by the anaesthetic and what slow agony it had been to wake up on the hospital bed, her body throbbing with loss. Having never described it to anyone, until she spoke to Diane she was convinced that no one else would have felt the same thing. The experience had been pushed way way down inside herself.

Later that night a man who was trying to pick Monica up told her a long and rambling story about how when he was a boy his best friend had disappeared and they had all eventually decided that he'd been kidnapped and was dead. Years later another boy from the same street ran into someone in Edinburgh who seemed too much like

Jeff for it to be a coincidence. He'd tried to find out as much as possible about this man, but the stranger was too reticent to give much away, a fact that made the other man all the more suspicious. Convinced that the person in Edinburgh was his long lost friend, he had come to the conclusion that, for some reason, Jeff had run away all those years ago. 'You know,' he said to Monica, 'I'd really like to see him again. Just to ask him why. Why did he run away? And where did he go?'

Monica went home alone that night. The next morning as she lay in the bath she thought about her new life. It looked good; her future was a blank page. Maybe she'd go to Spain with Diane and Siobhan. Diane had survived, so she should be able to as well. She had, she reminded herself, come from somewhere; she could edit her past but not deny it. With the abortion, something had ended. It was a most powerful metaphor for change.

Lois and The Ancients

———

Lois's life has been punctuated by Egyptian hieroglyphics. Its various stages have been marked by strange
involvements with cryptic designs from the ancient
people of the Nile. For Lois, the writing on the wall is
literally that of the blue Egyptian beetle, straight out of
the Book of the Dead.

There is a photograph of Lois that was taken during her
trip to Egypt. She is standing inside a tomb in the Valley
of the Kings. The photograph is very dark but the symbols
on the wall directly behind her are still visible. The
columns of pictographs end halfway up Lois's legs and
then, stretching across the wall, a banquet is depicted,
complete with naked serving girls ministering to those
dark, androgynous beauties who seem to have made up
the Egyptian ruling classes. On Lois's right in the photograph stands the boyfriend she was travelling with at the
time. He has struck what he considered to be a typical
ancient Egyptian pose: his arms and legs are all bent at
opposing angles, jutting out in a sort of bony and humor-
ous version of a swastika.

In this photograph Lois herself is peering at the camera.
She looks small, young, and like a tourist. She is sunburnt, round and very unlike the ancients who pose in
straight lines over her head, or the modern Egyptians who

wait patiently outside the tomb for her to pay them. Lois's affinity is with the symbols on the walls but it is not obvious in this or other photographs.

Lois has no Egyptian connections, as far as she knows. She is the granddaughter of farmworkers and history has never been one of her interests. She has no obvious link to the Book of the Dead. Ordinarily, Lois lives her life like most people and she is only very occasionally prone to acts of deviance. On a quiet Wednesday morning in the British Museum she once climbed into an Egyptian sarcophagus. She lay on her back on the cold timeless stone for a few brief moments before climbing back out.

The most serious problem in Lois's relatively problem-free life is that she has terrible trouble trying to find somewhere to live. The rental market dealing in small self-contained flats is out of her reach financially and the local housing bodies all see her as too single, too able, too young, and too uninsistent to house. So Lois has had to be content with the shifting, precarious, and increasingly less legal existence of a squatter. Her clothes, her bed, and her box of photographs and postcards from her one trip out of the country have moved with her from derelict property to boarded-up flat to unserviced nightmare and back again.

This unsettling lifestyle does not suit Lois at all. She is the kind of person who likes to know where she will be in three months' time, a not unusual personality trait, even amongst the young. Lois feels every time she gets her room sorted out, the photos and postcards stuck on the wall and her bed comfortably arranged, she has to pack it all up again and move on. This makes Lois nervous and unhappy.

'Let's move into this house,' Lois said to her friend Clara as they wandered around gazing into other people's warm sitting-rooms.

'Why this house?' asks Clara. She, too, is tired of moving.

'It looks nice. We could get in through the back. It probably has electricity and everything.'

'Who do you think owns it? We want to be careful this time. No more moving into empty houses that belong to that Duke, or Lord, or whatever he is. He'll have us out in an instant, just like before.'

'That's right. I don't think he owns anything around here though,' Lois said to Clara, staring up at the house's big windows, her eyes following the unbroken line of the guttering. She was trying to imagine what the house was like inside and what she would look like in it, what it would be like to live there. 'It's kind of posh around here, Clara. The pavements are so clean.'

'Mmm. The neighbours won't be used to squatters. They'll probably form a vigilante group and hound us out in the middle of the night, like the time before last.'

'No,' said Lois, 'that was the time before the time before.'

'Oh,' said Clara, 'well, that's probably what they'll do anyway.'

While Lois and Clara stood outside the house and talked they watched what went on in the quiet street. Eventually they decided to move into the house.

They got in through the back late that night, and then changed the lock of the front door. That took all night and so it was the next morning when Lois brought all her belongings to the house with the help of a friend with a van. Clara had put a piece of paper on the front door. It said. 'This property is legally occupied'.

Lois said to Clara, 'That sign will bring us to the attention of the neighbours. Let's take it down and hope they don't notice us. We only want to lead quiet lives, after all.'

'All right,' said Clara, and she went outside and took the sign down.

The house was very big and lovely with large, airy rooms and high ceilings. The services were all on and functioning and there were even carpets in one or two of the rooms. Everything about the house was in remarkably good shape, especially considering its age and that it had been empty for several years. Lois and Clara settled down to a springtime of home improvements. They did a bit of work on the garden and tried to dry out the basement which suffered from damp rising from no one knew where.

Without knowing who owned the house or what its fate, together with theirs, might be they worked on becoming more and more at home. Lois felt particularly attached to her bedroom. As the summer warmed up, her room remained cool, and there was always a sepulchral silence in it. The walls were panelled with dark heavy wood and were tremendously thick. Sunlight never fell on the north-facing rooms of the house, but they were well lit artificially. Lois felt happy there. She arranged her post-cards of mummies and sphinxes on the wall in a way that pleased her and, as the summer progressed and she spent more time in the garden, she began to take on that round and sunburnt look that she had had in the photograph, which she stuck on to her wall as well.

Late one night, Lois awoke suddenly. She sat up, turned her light on and looked around the room. Getting out of bed and putting on her clothes, she walked to the furthest wall in the room, the one adjacent to the windows where the fireplace must have been. Lois decided that it was time for the heavy wooden panelling to come off the walls. She went downstairs to find the hammer, crow-bar, and wedge, then she set about carefully prizing the panelling off the wall.

The panelling itself was very old; it had probably been on the walls for several hundred years. The nails were thick and square and the plaster of the wall beneath was solid. Lois strained and banged and pulled for a long time before the first panel gave slightly. Just as it was beginning to come away, Clara walked into the room.

'What are you doing Lois?' she asked, rubbing her eyes and yawning. 'It's terribly late. I thought we were still working on the basement. It seems a shame to start something new before we've finished down there.'

'I want to get rid of these panels. They're too dark,' Lois said, although she wasn't really sure why she was taking them down.

'Oh,' said Clara, 'I like those panels. We could have traded rooms; mine doesn't have any panelling.'

'No, I like this room, I want to stay in it. I don't like these panels though. You can have them after I take them down.' Lois was attempting to be very methodical and careful about removing the panels but, even so, as one came away there were splinters and sawdust.

'All right then,' Clara said walking out of the room. 'I'm going back to bed.'

A few minutes after Clara was gone, Lois succeeded in pulling the first panel off the wall. An enormous cloud of dust came out from underneath it, filling Lois's eyes and nose and smelling powerfully of the past. Lois kept working despite being unable to see properly and the panelling started to come away much more quickly once the first bit was removed. Every time she pulled a piece of the heavy wood away from the wall another large cloud of dust would come whooshing out. Lois got dirtier and dirtier and her eyes became reddened and sore. The smell grew stronger. It was a dry, musty smell that spoke of years of preservation, reminding Lois of something very particular that she could not quite place.

As soon as she got the last panel down Lois went off to have a bath, before the dust had settled. She shook herself out in the garden before getting into the warm water, then scrubbed her skin and shampooed her hair. Her body felt coated in dust and, despite her soaps and flannels, it continued to cling to her. Lois felt it was inside her body as well, filling her lungs and abdominal cavity. She drew the bath a second time and went through the whole process again. Once she had finished she felt marginally cleaner so she got out of the bath and dried herself off. She filled the tub again and dumped her clothes into it, then, clad in her towel, climbed the stairs back up to her bedroom. By then it was after dawn. Lois's entire room was covered in the thick disentombed dust: her bed, her clothes, the carpet. The smell was thick as well.

The panels were stacked in a pile where Lois had laid them, one by one, as she prized them away. The wall itself was there for Lois to gaze upon now. There were the vertical lines of hieroglyphics, scarab, bird, eye, lotus; there were the tall and slender men and women with that impenetrable, passive, and, at the same time, commanding expression on their faces; their sandled feet, their bejewelled ears and necks, their exquisitely long and lean arms stretching out towards the offerings of the naked serving girls or themselves making offerings to the mummies who were encased in gold and surrounded by jackal-headed minions.

Lois stood and looked at the wall for a long time, finally remembering where she had smelled the dust before. It was the same smell that hung in the air of the tombs in the Valley of the Kings. Ancient, dry, and scented ever so faintly with fragrant oils, paint, and gold: the smell of mummies and the wealthy dead. Lois went over to her bed and shook out the bedclothes. She climbed in underneath them and closed her eyes. In her last thoughts before she fell asleep she wondered who owned the house in which she was living and how long it would be before she and Clara were evicted.

Dreams From The Cold War

When Lizzie was a young girl she had a couple of friends who were sisters. They lived in a house that stood back-to-back with Lizzie's, separated by a very high and sturdy fence. The only way for Lizzie to visit Carrie and Cathy Rachov was by making a journey all the way around the block of houses, up her own street, along another street, and then down their street.

'Can you come over to play, Lizzie?' one of the sisters would shout. The girls communicated by standing in their respective gardens and yelling at each other over the fence.

'Yes, I'll ask my mum,' Lizzie would holler back, then run through her house, pausing briefly to ask her mum's permission.

Carrie and Cathy's house, although of exactly the same design as Lizzie's, seemed like another world. Mrs Rachov appeared to cook constantly and her food was unlike anything that Lizzie's mum made.

'My daddy', said Cathy one sunny day, 'escaped from the Soviet Union. He escaped from behind the Iron Curtain. He jumped over the Wall.'

'He did?' said Lizzie, her imagination captured. 'Why?'

'He wanted to be free of the Communist State,' said Cathy automatically. Lizzie took this information home

73

with her. At the dinner table she asked her parents about Carrie and Cathy's father. Lizzie's mother said, 'Oh the poor man. I bet he's glad to be in the West where he can raise his family as he pleases.' Lizzie thought about this and later at night while she lay in bed she thought about Mr Rachov escaping. As she began to get drowsy the Wall, the Iron Curtain, became the garden fence, tall and impenetrable. Just before she fell asleep she saw him, Mr Rachov, leaping over it like a gazelle.

While Lizzie was still a child one of her uncles left the country to emigrate to Canada. Because he was her father's youngest brother and Lizzie's favourite she had been allowed to sit up with him and her parents on the night before he left. She sat on his knee while the adults talked.

'I still don't understand why you are going, Hugh,' Lizzie's mother had said. 'It seems so far away and so, well, unlike home. You have no family there. It's all foreign.'

'I know Elizabeth, I know. Still, I don't want to stay here. They say things are changing for the better, but I'm not so sure. I don't want to bring up my children here.' At the time Lizzie thought this odd as Uncle Hugh didn't have any children.

'What do you mean Hugh?' her father said, sounding annoyed. 'It's a time of progress for us all.'

'Yeah, well, I don't like it. I'm leaving.'

'Oh Hugh, you make it sound like we're living in the Soviet Union!' Lizzie's mother exclaimed.

'Hmph,' Hugh snorted, 'at least then we'd have the vodka.'

'You've always been a bit of a Communist at heart Hugh, haven't you?' her mother said, not without affection.

Lizzie forgot about both of these incidents until she was grown-up and lived on her own, far away from her childhood friends. She'd been out of work for several months and had started having nightmares almost every night. One night she dreamed she was being chased down a dark alley. Every time she turned a corner around which she felt certain would be open space and freedom she would find a wall, high, smooth, and dark. She turned to face her pursuer and woke up.

The next night she dreamed that she was watching a military parade from a high concrete parapet. Wagner boomed through loudspeakers over the stands and massive flags flew from every building. The crowds cheered and slapped each other across the back as the tanks raised their guns and fired a ceremonious volley into the sky, startling the birds and waking her up.

On another night Lizzie dreamed she was enrolled at a foreign university. Attempting to get to know the other students and make herself at home proved difficult; the other students seemed reluctant to talk to Lizzie. She discovered, quite by accident, that they had developed a secret weapon so hideous that the enemy spies hadn't taken it seriously. The students had happened upon a certain chemical manufactured in the human brain that, when combined with another chemical injected intravenously, enabled people to produce an ultra-violet beam of light. This beam shot out through the human mouth and was capable of incinerating anything in its way. The students realised Lizzie had stumbled upon their discovery and, as a particularly good-looking boy with laser-blue eyes came towards her, opening his mouth, she awoke.

During the daytime, Lizzie looked for work. While riding the bus back and forth across town she tried to read the newspaper but found her mind constantly returning to her dreams from the previous nights.

Lost in a huge city, Lizzie ran from doorway to doorway feeling certain that she was being followed. She rounded a corner and found herself on the edge of an enormous square that stretched out in front of her as flat and peopleless as the Siberian tundra. Knowing that she must cross this square on her own, she took a few steps. A loud keening noise filled the sky. She turned around quickly but was now in the middle of the square and it seemed miles back to the relative safety of the city's narrow alleyways. Turning once again, she found herself at the base of a colossal statue. By craning her neck Lizzie saw that the statue depicted a goddess of war. Suddenly the statue began to move, the draped torso swinging forward as its right foot left the ground. The dark night grew darker as the foot of the colossus came towards Lizzie. She turned over in bed and woke up.

Lizzie was at what seemed to be a large demonstration with hundreds and thousands of other people. She stood in the middle of a large square surrounded by people who were shouting and applauding. Suddenly a dark cloud came overhead and she saw, in the distance, the police surge forward. The crowd pressed backwards as the police marched ahead, some on horseback, all carrying plexiglass shields and batons and even guns. People began to scream, turning to run. They came towards Lizzie in a great mass, their mouths open in silent shouts. She felt her knees go weak and as the crowd came running she collapsed on the ground. When the first feet reached her she woke up and, once again, headed out to look for work.

One evening while having dinner with her parents Lizzie said, 'Maybe I should emigrate like Uncle Hugh.'

'Whatever for dear?' asked her mother. 'I can't imagine where you'd go.'

'I keep having horrible nightmares. I'm worried about money.'

'Hmmph,' said her father. 'No wonder. Why can't you find work?'

'I don't know, Dad,' replied Lizzie. 'There just isn't any.'

'You've been left out in the cold,' her mum said, shaking her head.

'It's the cold war,' replied Lizzie, 'I've been shut out.'

The Unbearable Shortness of Holidays

In Perugia all sensibility is lost. It floats away on the warm sectarian breeze that drifts up from the South becoming thinner and thinner as it crosses Europe. For the out-of-town, out-of-country visitor this hill-top town, surrounded by rich and fragrant farmland, can seem like nirvana.

'Ah,' sighed the tourist, 'there is no hurly-burly here.'

'Mmm,' sighed the other tourist, 'the only hustle is the evening rounds of the cafés and even then one can always find a seat.'

'Mmm.' The two tourists were in reflective mode, which they termed as the Italian mode. 'Somewhere someone must be working,' said one tourist to the other as she opened her lazy eyes and took a languid look around. 'But I can't see who.'

'Well,' the other replied, 'it's not me.' They both sighed again and went back to sleep over their Cinzano in the mid-day sun.

In Perugia the tourist need not be intrepid to discover the joys of the local environs. The cafés, bars and restaurants are easy to find; the atmosphere lulls without any effort. The wine is in the shops, the smell of flowers in the air, the doors of the churches open, and the lanes and byways are to be walked through. There is even a Roman aqueduct, conveniently placed across the fuchsia-laden slope. You don't have to look for anything – an indolent tourist's dream come true.

The day began like this: six o'clock, it was sunny, Elena woke up. The pigeons were cooing loudly, a cool breeze came through the shutters on the window. 'My God,' Elena thought, 'another day here. Another day away from my job. Another day to drink Campari and wear dark glasses and smile. My God.' She lay still in her narrow bed listening to the morning sounds that drifted through her window.

In the next bed Lucia lay sleeping. The two women had adopted Italian names for the duration of the holiday. In fact, Lucia was dreaming that she was an Italian running through a field of mimosa. At one end of the field a small village fair was taking place. There was only one table at the fair. It was draped with a banner that read, 'The Revolutionary Communist Party of Italy'. The table was laden with food. The Italian communists were selling Gnocchi alla Gorgonzola – little balls of heaven smothered in blue, briny delight. Lucia smiled in her sleep.

After another hour the two women had risen and were making their way through the morning rituals of showering and dressing. Elena kept collapsing on to the bed with her copy of *L'Uomo*, a men's fashion magazine. Lucia was trying to read Shelley but found she could not concentrate whatever the time of day, the lazy morning, the quiet afternoon, nor the peaceful evening. Every day in the café she would bring out her book and begin to read. 'Many a green isle needs must be/In the deep wide sea of Misery', and every day she yawned and stretched and looked up from her book at the people passing by.

'Elena,' she said, 'I can't concentrate on anything, not even a poem.'

'No,' said Elena, who didn't attempt to read, 'there's too much to look at, smell and drink.'

After dressing, the two women floated out of their pensione and wandered over to the coffee bar where they ate custard-filled pastries and drank cappuccino, weak tea and juice for breakfast. They stood inside the coffee bar while they ate, alongside the older men, cloth-capped and short, and the younger women who were smartly dressed for business. The tourists' eyes were steamed open by the coffee machine which hissed and puffed as they stood without speaking, listening to the morning conversation around them. What did the words these Italians used mean as they flew back and forth over the sleepy heads of Elena and Lucia? The elderly man in the felt vest – was he talking about the weather which was perfect, or the coffee which was aromatic, or the day ahead which to Elena and Lucia seemed magical? Or was he talking about politics and the strength of the Italian economy, 'Il Sorpasso', the money in the North and the poverty in the South? And what did he do during the war?

Elena was nodding off over her coffee so Lucia suggested they get another cup from the busy man behind the coffee bar and move to one of the rickety tables outside. There they sat in the morning sun, Elena napping behind her dark glasses, Lucia examining an English newspaper.

'Home has never looked so bleak,' Lucia said to Elena. 'I can't imagine why I live there.' Elena, looking up, let her dark glasses slide to the tip of her nose so she could peer over them at Lucia.

'You live there, Lucia, because it is home,' she replied, pushing her dark glasses back up on to the bridge of her nose.

'Yes, of course, it is home. But it does seem terrible from here. Look at this weather report. It has been raining all week and will continue to rain all next week. The government is introducing austerity to the poor – isn't that a bit

like introducing the Pope to God? Look at this Elena, look
at this,' Lucia said, holding up the newspaper and pointing at the headline, MASS SUICIDE ON LONDON BRIDGE:
TWENTY BROKERS DEAD. Can you explain that?'

'They'd probably been caught fiddling or something,'
Elena replied. 'I wonder how high the suicide rate is
here?'

'Suicide?' she laughed. 'In heaven?' She shook her
head.

'Lucia,' Elena said firmly, lowering her dark glasses
once more. 'One tourist's heaven can be a resident's hell.'

'Hmm,' muttered Lucia folding up her newspaper and
resolving not to buy another. After sipping her coffee she
cleared her throat and, simultaneously, cleared her mind
of unemployment, racism, and decline.

Elena and Lucia spent their days repeating a seemingly
endless cycle of enormously pleasurable activities. They
would rise, breakfast, and then spend the morning
wandering around Perugia with their mouths open. They
looked in the shops, toured the churches, wandered along
the hillside spotting remnants of the Etruscan city from a
time before. They sniffed the scented breeze and followed
their noses to a shop where they bought food for a picnic
lunch: olives, artichokes, marinated tomatoes, bread, Gorgonzola and Orvieto vino bianco secco. Then they'd find a
park or a piece of grass in a churchyard where they would
sit in the sun and eat and drink and maybe chat to other
tourists while quietly and slowly falling asleep. The
mid-day zephyr would play along the hem of Elena's
skirt, sliding up her leg like a warm hand. Lucia dreamed
of Mario Lanza; she could hear 'Ave Maria' in her
sleep.

After a while they gathered their things and walked
back up to the town centre, climbing the narrow steps that
wind up through the buildings, past medieval churches
and under Etruscan arches. Perugia is like that, all up and
down, steps instead of streets; there is a lift that travels

from one part of town up on the hill to another part down below. The tourist stumbles upon sudden views; rounding a corner you are greeted by the valley and surrounding hills. They call out to you like a dream of Italy, too lovely to be real. The poplars stand straight like boy soldiers; the tourist can lead an enchanted life, not like home at all.

Back in the huge cobbled square that forms the town centre Lucia and Elena would spend the rest of the afternoon sitting in one of the six or seven outdoor cafés that line the square. They'd nibble on bar snacks and drink Cinzano and Campari and aqua minerale and coffee whilst attempting to read or write on postcards. They'd speak in broken English to the people at the next table, foreigners studying at the University for Strangers, one of the city's institutes of learning. Elena felt that she wanted to move to Perugia and be a stranger at the university herself.

The afternoon sun shone down on the town square. Lucia hiked her dress up, exposing her brown legs. 'Elena,' she said, 'I don't want to go home.'

'Neither do I, neither do I.'

'Maybe we could ring up our bosses and tell them we're not coming back. We could ring our banks and have them transfer our accounts to the Bank of Perugia. We could find someone to move into our flats. Then we could stay here forever. Growing old in Perugia, Elena, we won't get rheumatism here! We won't end up starving on tiny pensions. Oh, oh, we can be Italians and wear dark glasses and study Gramsci and discuss Fellini and eat fettucini Alfredo until we die!'

Elena opened her eyes. 'Lucia,' she said, 'this is a holiday. We are tourists. Life isn't like this, Italy isn't like this. How would we live, we'd have to get jobs, who'd be our friends, what about our responsibilities?' Elena sighed and shook her head slowly in the afternoon sun. 'We're tourists here.' Lucia sighed then as well, feeling great sadness as she stared into her Martini bianco. Life seemed so perfect.

The afternoon became early evening and the two women left the café and walked back to the pensione. Once again, they showered and dressed with the windows wide open on to the sunset. The smell of cooking floated up from a kitchen nearby as they headed off to find a restaurant for dinner. Lucia and Elena would spend a good hour examining menus and debating about where they should eat.

'Bruschetta,' said Elena. 'I demand bruschetta. It's bruschetta or nothing, I swear!'

'Mmm,' said Lucia, 'I want zucchini. I want tortellini. I want it all!' Eventually, they settled on somewhere and had a long and drawn-out meal, arguing with the people at the next table while being either charmed or ignored by the waiters. Around midnight they made their way home, giggling as they tripped on the cobblestones, stopping for gelati on the way. The next day they woke up early and everything began again.

Eventually, the day came when the return flight was scheduled to take off and no matter how much they objected, swearing to the skies and cursing the great God of Work, they were on it, like dutiful daughters.

The next year Elena and Lucia met in a London pub to plan their forthcoming holiday. It was a dark and raining February night.

'Well, where shall we go this year my dear?' Elena asked Lucia.

'To Italy, of course!' replied Lucia, shocked by Elena's question which she felt implied there was an alternative. 'We'll go to Perugia.'

'Again?' said Elena.

'What do you mean, "again"?' said Lucia, her voice full of surprise and hurt.

'Well, we could go to Greece and sun ourselves amongst the ruins, or we could go to Spain and eat paella, or even

Portugal, I hear it's nice and not crowded.'

'But what about the cafés in the town square? What about our walks on the hills? Our day trips to Lago Trasimere?' Lucia stared into her pint of beer moodily. Two months later she and Elena were on the plane, heading for, ultimately, Perugia.

When they arrived they found the very same little pensione where they'd stayed the previous year. The first evening they went back to their favourite restaurant where the head waiter recognised them, greeting them by name. Lucia smiled broadly at Elena once they were seated.

'Ah, it is paradise. Aren't you pleased that I was so keen to come back? We'll have a wonderful fortnight, I know it.'

'Yes,' replied Elena. 'We will.' They spent the evening lingering over a tremendous meal and then stopped for gelati as they stumbled home.

In the morning, they awoke early as the birds began to sing and the first rays of sun broke through. The sounds of the town filtered up into their room. Lucia stretched her limbs out on the bed. Elena was already up, getting ready for a shower.

'I think,' said Lucia, 'I think I'll have a gelato for breakfast.'

'A what?' replied Elena, aghast.

'A gelato, Elena. I want a gelato for breakfast. A pink one. Then we can go and have the brioche and coffee like we always do.'

'A gelato,' said Elena thoughtfully. 'Well, why not? You're on holiday, you can have whatever you want!'

So the two women set off to find Lucia ice-cream for breakfast. Luckily, one eager entrepreneur had antici-pated this foreigner's early morning urge for sweetness and had opened his gelato counter at dawn. Lucia asked him for a pink one, a triple, and they sat on the steps of the medieval town hall while she ate it. The sun grew steadily stronger while the two women made their way to a coffee bar where they stood in the steam of the espresso machine and drank cups of hot coffee and ate brioche. They spent the morning reacquainting themselves with Perugia and then, as before, bought themselves the ingredients of a picnic for lunch. Taking a bus out of town, they disembarked at the first poppy-covered hill they saw and, sitting in the shade of a Lombardy poplar, ate.

'The air is so soft,' Lucia said, 'it's like ice-cream. Soft and smooth and delicious.'

'Ice-cream?' said Elena, slightly annoyed. 'But ice-cream is cold and here the air is so warm.'

'Like warm ice-cream then,' replied Lucia, her head tilted back and her face in the sun. 'Melted.'

They spent the afternoon dozing on the hillside, listening to the sounds of the country. In the distance a farmer was toiling. He glanced their way from time to time.

At about half-past four they arose and began to walk back into Perugia. Three-quarters of the way there Lucia said, 'When we get back into town, do you know what I'd like?'

'A Cinzano,' said Elena greedily. 'Or maybe a Campari. Vino bianco. Vino rosso . . . vino . . .'

'A gelato,' interrupted Lucia. 'A green one.' Then she smiled to herself, a large benevolent grin, the fat smile of a happy woman.

'And you shall have it, I decree,' replied Elena. When they reached the town they wandered towards the centre through the cobblestone byways and up the narrow staircases. Then they found a table at a café in the town square. When the waiter came over to them, Elena asked for a Martini bianco secco and Lucia asked for gelato, the green kind, in a dish with whipped cream. They sat in the late-afternoon sun and laughed at each other.

The next morning after they'd showered and dressed and were on their way to breakfast, Lucia made a slight detour into the corner shop where she persuaded the proprietor, with broken Italian and much gesticulating, to sell her a gelato. Elena had assumed that Lucia had gone into the shop for something much more basic, like tampons or tissues, but tried not to show her surprise. Lucia ate the ice-cream like a starved person as they walked in the direction of the coffee bars.

The same thing happened on the way to their lunchtime picnic and then, as they were making a tour of the restaurant menus trying to decide where to have their evening meal, Lucia slipped away while Elena was musing over the tortellini and came back licking a gelato. A blue one this time.

'Lucia!' exclaimed Elena, alarmed. 'Another gelato?'

'So?' she replied defensively. 'Another gelato, so what? I like them. Do you mind?'

'Not at all, my dear, but it would spoil my appetite.'

'Well, it doesn't spoil mine,' answered Lucia. 'Not one bit.'

Over the course of the next couple of days Lucia ate more Italian ice-cream than most Italians would eat in a month, maybe even a year. She ate all the flavours of gelati she could find then she began to comb the city for more. Pistachio, lemon, orange, fruit, coffee, rum, chocolate, amaretto, strawberry, peach, chocolate-chip, blueberry, blackberry, and all the alcoholic varieties: Lucia was compiling a mental list. On the occasions she was unable to find a new flavour she was not put off, but would take the opportunity to reassess what she'd thought of it the first time.

Elena watched with increasing dismay. She tried to curb her friend's new habit with subtlety at first.

'Too much sugar is not good for your skin,' she said gently.

To which Lucia replied, 'So what?'

'Too many dairy products are not good for your blood or your digestion.'

To which Lucia replied, 'Bollocks.'

'You'll get ice-cream gag,' she tried one afternoon mid-gelato, 'and then you'll never want to eat it again.'

'No way,' replied Lucia. 'That will never happen to me. I love it too much.'

'You're telling me,' whispered Elena under her breath.

In the early evening of the fourth day when Lucia was about to embark on her sixth gelato of the day, Elena could stand it no longer. 'YOU'LL GET FAT!' she shouted as loudly as she could.

'I DON'T CARE!' shouted Lucia back.

The next morning Elena packed up her belongings and moved to another room in the pensione. She began to tour Perugia and the environs on her own. She took a day-trip to Florence and stood and stared at Michelangelo's David for several hours. She travelled around the countryside swimming in the gentle lakes and walking over the quiet hills. One day she went to Assisi to see the frescoes of Giotto. There she met an Englishman who offered to buy her a gelato. She thanked him but said no and took the bus back to Perugia. Then she went looking for her friend.

Lucia was seated at a café in the square. She'd grown quite brown in the days since Elena had seen her last. In front of her on the table was a large silver bowl full of ice-cream, fruit and whipped cream. When Elena spotted her she was poised to dive into it with a big silver spoon.

'Hello there,' said Elena. 'How are you?'

Lucia dropped her spoon. It fell into the whipped cream and disappeared like a plane flying into a cloud. She looked up at Elena and then back down at the ice-cream. 'Hello,' she said without looking back up. 'Where did it go?'

'Look,' said Elena assertively. 'I've got something to say to you.'

'Oh don't bother. I know what it is already. Well, I'm not going home this time. I'm not going back to that dark mucky place. The ice-cream is lousy there.'

'I'm not asking you to come back,' said Elena. 'What I'm

asking is why. Why are you doing it this way? You could have found a quicker way.'

'A quicker way to what?' asked Lucia, looking up. 'A quicker way to eat ice-cream?'

'No, a quicker way to freeze time,' she replied.

Lucia looked back down at her ice-cream. The swirls of colour, cheerful bits of fruit, and mountains of whipped cream looked heavenly to her. In the ice-cream she could see a better world, one that would fit her, that she could eat up and feel happy in. In gelato there is certainty, a priceless commodity in a post-modern world. 'I don't want it to melt away,' she said to Elena who remained impassive behind her dark glasses.

'Neither do I, Lucia, neither do I.'

The Fact-Finding Mission

Dora came home and found the note on the kitchen table. It said, in large bold letters, THE ENGLISH ARE REPRESSED BECAUSE THEY HAVE NO LAKES. Dora sighed when she read this and wondered if it was true. There are a few lakes, somewhere, but they are all kept in the Lake District, as if one can't allow lakes just anywhere. If lakes are not kept where they belong everyone might start throwing off their clothes and jumping in and we all know where that would lead.

Dora sighed and sat down. She was very tired. She had been out on one of her fact-finding missions. As usual, she had found there were no facts to find. 'One day,' thought Dora, 'one day I'll give up my search and then where will we all be?' She sighed again, then picked up the note and turned it over. On the other side it said, THE ENGLISH ARE REPRESSED BECAUSE THEY HAVE NO MOUNTAINS. 'No mountains and no lakes,' thought Dora. 'How true.' She slumped off to bed.

In the morning Dora got up, not at all refreshed, and set off on one of her fact-finding missions again. Dora strove to find facts nearly every day now. She felt she was being driven mad by misinformation. 'There are so many lies everywhere,' she often said. 'They are lying about everything these days. Wars, identities, deaths. I can't believe

anything. I must seek out the facts. I must find out the
truth.'

Dora knew she was being a bit ridiculous, but she was
unemployed so that kind of thing didn't matter to her.
Besides, when she set out on her fact-finding missions
she felt really terrific, like Simone de Beauvoir, or Mrs
Emma Peel, or Isabelle Bird. She'd put on her favourite
clothes and pretend the No. 77 bus was a Bat-bus and that
her umbrella had a gun in it. Not that Dora would ever
actually try to shoot anyone. Well, no one, except of
course, The Liars, if she could find them, wherever and
whoever they are.

Dora took the No. 77 bus up the Strand and got out in
front of the High Court. She already knew there were no
truths, or facts, there but she went anyway, from time to
time, just in case. As she was about to head through the
doors, she spotted a note on the wall. It said, YOU HATE
THE NEW TELECOM PHONE KIOSKS MERELY
BECAUSE YOU ARE RESISTANT TO CHANGE. On reading this Dora knew she would not find any facts that day,
so she gave up before she had started and walked down
the Strand towards Waterloo Bridge, where there are no
facts, only sandwich bars and shops selling briefcases.

Dora had been unemployed for a rather long time. She
was very poor and her activities were restricted for the
most part to listening to the radio, fact-finding missions,
talking to friends and other free or very cheap things, like
walking in the rain, making up theories about her com-
patriots, and worrying. She did a lot of the latter. Her
friends in work found her increasingly difficult. No one
could understand these fact-finding missions.

'Except the person or persons who keep leaving me
those notes,' said Dora aloud in the kitchen. She sighed
heavily. 'When will I find the place where the facts are?
When will I discover where the truth is kept? In the same
place as they keep the jobs, I'll bet.' She decided to go and
see one of her friends.

Dora went to visit Nora, who lived just around the corner. Nora had also been unemployed for a very long time and she had recently decided to give up applying for jobs and devote her life to the pursuit of complete happiness. This did not involve happiness-finding missions, but it did involve a lot of soul-searching and some heavy-duty reading. Nora was slowly realising that she could not actually afford anything that she thought would give her complete happiness, like a trip to the Soviet Union, for example.

'Oh Nora,' said Dora, 'you're so materialistic. Happiness is one of the free things.'

'Shut up Dora,' screamed Nora, 'it is not! Happiness costs lots and lots of money, and besides, wanting to fly to Rio isn't materialistic. Don't try to tell me that your fact-finding missions make you happy. I have the ease in life, but none of the good things to enjoy in that ease. I have the leisure, but none of the leisurables. I can't even afford to play squash!'

'Oh Nora,' said Dora, 'Don't be so miserable. I didn't know you were so miserable. If only I could tell you the facts. If only I could explain things.'

'Dora,' said Nora, 'you're a real dreamer. Even more of a dreamer than I am. At least I'm trying to pursue something that will get me somewhere.'

'Oh,' said Dora. She felt rather depressed. She got up and kissed Nora on the cheek and then left. As she was unlocking her bicycle, she saw the note taped to the cross-bar. It said, THE ARISTOCRACY IS EXPANDING AT THE SPEED OF LIGHT. Dora got on her bicycle and rode home.

When Dora got home, she took a bath. As she lay there in the hot water, she thought about Nora and what she had said that morning. Dora didn't think Nora was being very realistic.

'How can you find complete happiness if you don't know the facts? How could you ever be sure that what it was that gave you complete happiness wasn't, in fact, something horrible and monstrous? Factually unsubstantiated happiness would be so risky: any day you might find out the facts and bang your happiness would be gone.' Dora submerged herself in the bath water. She wished she understood things better.

When Dora got out of the bath she found a note pinned to her towel. It said, ALL HISTORY IS THE SAME: RUTHLESS, BITTER, AND MEANINGLESS. 'Ha!' thought Dora, 'is that a fact?' She dried herself off and went into her room and tried to plan the next day's fact-finding missions. But she was running low on ideas and decided to get back into the bath. When she got out of the bath again, quite a while later, there was another note pinned to her towel. It said, THE UNEMPLOYED WRINKLE MORE EASILY THAN THE EMPLOYED.

Dora got up the next day and thought about what she should do. So far that month she'd been to The City, Highgate Cemetery, The Granville Arcade, Southwark Town Hall, The British Library, Hyper-Hyper, the Centrale Café, 'Cats', several branches of W.H. Smith, Kennington Police Station, the Polytechnic of Central London, and many, many other places, each of which had seemed potential and, in some cases, promising fact-sources until Dora actually investigated them. At the end of each mission she was always forced to conclude the same thing: that facts are, indeed, elusive little items.

So, Dora decided she would ride the Circle Line until she found the truth. She got on at Victoria and began to circle central London hoping to pick up some facts rather like a vulture circles its prey. At Paddington she noticed the note stuck on the window behind her. It said, THERE IS NO SUCH THING AS A FACT; ALL THAT EXISTS IS ABSOLUTE FICTION.

Dora read this note and then read it again. She sat on her seat on the Circle Line train and wondered if the note was true. If it was true it meant that she would now have nothing to do every day, no mission in life, no reason to get up. So, Dora chose to ignore it, as people ignore even the most obvious of messages. The Circle Line carried Dora away from Paddington Station. And then, eventually, it brought her back again.

The Moose

———

She arrived by aeroplane on a sunny January day at lunchtime. They flew in over British Columbia, a province which consists of endless mountain ranges, logging developments, and small towns nestled in the valleys. As the plane flew further north distances between the increasingly tiny towns became greater and the landscape grew more vast and impressive. Irene felt glad to be leaving the South behind. She had been up to the North before and imagined she knew what it was like: empty and mysterious, more legends and myths than people. The North is the last frontier in Canada, consistently unconquerable.

The plane landed on the small Whitehorse runway. As everyone stood stretching, yawning, and reaching for their parkas and sheepskin coats, Irene shivered. The doors of the plane were opened and they piled on to the tarmac. Once out in the sharp, clean air she breathed in slowly and, with a shock, felt the hair and skin in her nose and throat freeze. She breathed out again quickly and, with relief, felt them thaw.

The sunlight was brilliant and blinding as it reflected on the windows of the terminal. The air itself was prickly, as if full of ice crystals, and very dry in contrast to the bog-like climate of Vancouver. She followed the crowd, none of whom seemed to be alarmed by respiration problems as they were herded into the building.

Irene was able to recognise the man who had come to meet her as he was holding a sign bearing her name, 'Irene Jacobs'. The man was very large and wore a huge grey parka that reached his knees.

'Hello,' said Irene.

'Hello,' he said. 'I'm Harry. Do you want some coffee? Was your flight all right? We'll need to wait a bit for the bags.'

'Yes,' Irene replied. 'I'd like some coffee. The flight was fine.' She paused and then asked, 'What's the temperature here today?'

'Oh, it's not very cold, only −20°C or so. It's warmed up a bit since last week. We had a fortnight's stretch of −40°C. Haven't you ever been here before?'

'No,' replied Irene.

'You're in for a shock,' replied Harry, laughing. Irene felt stupid, new, and uninitiated.

'When was the last time you were in the South?' Irene asked Harry as she sipped her coffee.

'Well, my wife and I went to Edmonton last year and we're going Outside again next month. We try to get Outside once a year. Mind you, we're always glad to come home. It gets weirder and weirder out there, I swear.' If the rest of the world is 'Outside', thought Irene, then it follows that the Yukon must be the 'Inside' making it sound like an exclusive club, or perhaps, a prison.

By the time Irene's bags arrived in the terminal and she and Harry were heading towards the truck, it was almost 1.30 p.m. and the sun was going down.

'The days are short here,' Irene commented.

'No,' Harry said, 'the sun just goes down early and comes up late. Still have to be at work at 7.00 a.m.' They drove out of the airport and along the ridge, then took the road down into town.

Whitehorse lies in a valley on the banks of the Yukon

river. On the colder winter days when the rest of the Yukon sky is clear this valley fills with ice-fog, frozen exhaust mingled with wood smoke from the town's cars and houses. As Harry and Irene headed into town it became increasingly difficult to see but Harry seemed to know where to go.

'We'll just pick up the kids and head out to the house,' he said. 'I've got to get back down here for a meeting.'

'OK,' said Irene as they drove past houses that looked warm and friendly, nestled close together in the snow. 'Why is it so hard to see?'

'Ice-fog.'

'Oh. What's that?'

'It's what people get lost in,' said Harry looking at Irene out of the corner of his eye. After a couple of minutes they pulled into a driveway. Getting out of the car, Irene followed Harry through a door in the side of the house. Inside they met a woman who pointed towards two small boys and said, 'These are Barry and Bobby. Barry doesn't like to eat much and Bobby, well, he's very sweet.' The woman shook Irene's hand firmly and said, 'Good luck.'

Barry and Bobby were already bundled into their parkas, gloves, hats, scarves and boots so Harry and Irene carried them out to the truck. The children sat in between the adults on the big, wide seat, so heavily dressed they could hardly move. Irene envied them, it wasn't just the little hairs inside her nose that were freezing. Harry backed the truck down the drive and began to head out of town.

'Hello,' she said to Barry and Bobby. 'How old are you Barry?'

'Four,' he said. Irene smiled.

'How old are you Bobby?'

'Baby doesn't talk,' said Barry. 'He's only one.'

'Oh,' she replied, unable to think of what to say next. Harry was watching her.

They sat in silence for about ten miles. The truck

climbed back up the hill and turned on to the highway
that ran along the ridge. Irene stared out the window into
the darkness. Occasionally they'd pass some form of life
on the side of the road, a garage and café, a rather well-lit
junkyard, the odd house. The road was fairly straight,
slightly hilly, and unpaved but so frozen it was smooth.

'I wish we were doing this in the daytime so I could see
where we are going,' Irene said to Harry who was
absorbed by the driving.

'There's not much to see,' he answered. 'Just skinny
trees and big dogs and dead animals on the side of the
road.'

'Oh,' said Irene. Barry and Bobby seemed to be asleep.
Wondering if they had suffocated under their bulky
wrappings, she leant over to have a better look at them.
But both boys were breathing and Bobby was actually
awake. He looked at her silently with large brown eyes.

'Hello,' she said. He smiled.

After another ten miles or so of the same untenanted
landscape, they turned off the main road and headed into
the trees. 'This is Wolf Creek,' said Harry. 'This is where
the house is. I'll take you in and show you how everything works. Then I'll have to go back into town.'

'OK by me,' Irene said cheerfully. 'This is going to be
fun.' She stared out of the window at the moonlit trees.
Irene could hear Harry's beard scrape against his parka
as he turned his head to look at her.

The drive up to the house was long and narrow, a badly
cared for road full of holes and paved with ice. Harry
drove up it confidently and when they reached the dark
house swung the truck around.

'Here we are kids,' she said, opening the door. Irene
unbuckled Bobby's seat belt, lifted him out and carried
him up an icy set of wooden steps that led to the door of
the house while Harry followed behind with the keys.
Irene went inside and fumbled to find the light, but
before she could, it was on and there stood Barry saying,

'It's over here. This is my house.' Smiling sourly Irene went back outside to get her bags.

Once everything had been brought inside Harry led Irene around showing her all the switches and taps and giving instructions on how to work the appliances. They went down into the basement and Harry stopped in front of the furnace.

'This is your lifeline,' he said. 'Without it you and those boys will freeze. It's a wood-burning furnace: you see these logs?' He pointed to a large and neat pile of trees, denuded of branches and bark, that sat in the corner. 'The furnace requires one of these every few hours or several of them a couple of times a day. You open this door', he said, opening it and giving her a brief glimpse of hell, 'and shove them in head first. Don't forget.'

After a few more brief explanations Harry said, 'Well, I'm off. My number is beside the phone in case you need any help. There's a note from Barry and Bobby's mum there too. They'll be back in the afternoon a week from tomorrow. Good luck.' He smiled and was gone, leaving Irene alone with the boys.

The house was based on the A-frame design but with extra bits attached so it was more like an M-frame. The bedrooms were up in the peaks of the roof with small triple-glazed windows and thick carpet. The kitchen was well-equipped and stocked with enough food for a month. The back room, the one they had come in through, was full of boots, skis, a sled, a toboggan and other winter necessities. The freezer was also in this room and Irene opened it to find what looked like an entire moose hacked up and frozen in small packages. On the wall above the freezer hung several rifles.

Wandering through the house, Irene went into the sitting-room and found Barry and Bobby sitting in front of the television. They were watching a rerun of 'The Munsters', thumbs set firmly in their mouths. The sitting-room had several comfy chairs, a sofa, a dining-table and a piano. The room took up most of the front of the M: the walls sloped up to a high point and the huge, curtainless windows looked out onto the trees making the house feel very exposed. Reflected in the window were Barry and Bobby, their faces made blue by the light of the television. Beyond them there was nothing.

Irene turned around and surveyed the rest of the room. On the wall above the entrance to the kitchen hung the head of a moose, its great set of antlers still intact. He stared down with huge, limpid, brown, moose eyes set into a big, rounded, moose head. Irene thought he looked sad and slightly dopey. She could imagine him standing in the wild outside the window, his enormous warm bulk held up by skinny legs and knobbly knees.

'Bullwinkle,' she said out loud. 'You'll keep me company.'

'What?' said Barry with his thumb still in his mouth.

'Nothing,' she replied. 'Are you hungry?'

'No,' said Barry.

'Oh. Well maybe Bobby is.'

'Yep. Baby's always hungry.' On hearing that Bobby took his thumb out of his mouth and, pulling his eyes away from Herman Munster, smiled at Irene. She walked back into the kitchen.

In the Yukon, there are two seasons: summer, which is light and windy with 24-hour daylight, and winter, which is long, dark, and formidable. In between there are very brief and violent intervals when everything either freezes or thaws overnight. The time elsewhere known as 'spring' is particularly shocking. The thaw sets in and, suddenly, the rock-hard ground becomes thick with disgusting muck, capable of swamping a four-wheel drive. The frost recedes and the permafrost is prone to the heaves, accomplishing herculean feats like picking up a large stretch of hitherto straight road and throwing it thirty-five feet to the left. The most extraordinary spectacle by far is when the rivers break up. The ice, which may be many feet thick, begins to crack and move down river producing a terrifying cacophony of noise; groaning, screeching, and crashing. To newcomers it may appear that Armageddon has arrived.

But when Irene landed in the Yukon it was mid-January and spring was far away. Like most good Canadians, she knew all about the North, but had never seen it. She came to the Yukon to make money and thought of babysitting Barry and Bobby as the first step. To her the North was a foreign land where if she couldn't get rich by mining gold, she could at least make a good living by serving beer to those who were.

On her first day, daylight had come and gone in the space of a few hours. There was no wind and no snow and the temperature could drop at any moment to well below −40°C where it might stay for days on end. Whitehorse itself remains quite lively in January, the bars are busy until late at night and people go about business undeterred. But to Irene, twenty miles out of town, in a big house with two small children, surrounded by trees and perpetual darkness, it seemed as though the world had stopped and there was no one else left alive. It was definitely more than she'd bargained for. And so unbelievably quiet as well.

That first evening Barry wouldn't eat anything so she fed Bobby and read them both a long story.

'That's dumb,' Barry said, 'things just don't happen that way. Can I watch television?'

'No,' said Irene, 'read a book.'

'No,' replied Barry. 'When's my mummy coming back? I don't like you.' Bobby tugged at Irene's sweater. When she looked down at him, he smiled.

After putting them to bed and stoking the furnace, a task she was not about to forget, Irene turned the television back on. Being so far from anywhere meant that the only channel available was the CBC and whatever was on looked dull, so she turned it off. She sat with the lights on and stared at the window, wishing there were curtains to pull. In the reflection she could see the head of the moose. He was staring at her staring at him in the window. Beyond that was the dark night.

They spent the next morning colouring and when the sun came up Irene announced to the children that they were going for a walk. Barry became impatient while she was putting on Bobby's coat, boots, and all the other clothes that he needed in order to survive the elements. She carried the small boy outside, down the stairs, and then went back to fetch the sled.

The sun was shining and the air was crisp and cold. Irene became used to it quickly as the inside of her nose froze and thawed with reassuring regularity. They walked past the big windows of the sitting-room and headed out through the trees. It was tough going as there was little snow, lots of broken branches and stubby sawn-off stumps blocking the path of the sled.

'I'm cold,' said Barry.

'We'll warm up as we walk,' Irene replied.

'No we won't,' he retorted, 'it's too cold to warm up just like that.'

'Look at that tree Barry, isn't it a strange shape? What does it remind you of?' She pointed to an oddly bent tree on the left.

'Nothing,' said Barry. They struggled on through the woods. The sun shone weakly as they passed skinny tree after skinny tree. They seemed to go on forever.

'Where are we going?' asked Barry. 'I'm bored.'

'OK,' said Irene, 'we'll go back.' She felt relieved; she was beginning to think they'd get lost. Her feet were cold, her cheeks were smarting, and the landscape was a little too empty. They made a swoop around a couple of trees and headed back the way they had come, which was, in fact, hardly any distance at all. The house was less than one hundred yards away. As they struggled back towards it Irene heard a quiet thud behind her. Turning around she saw that Bobby had fallen off the sled. He was lying on his back with his arms and legs spread out around him, too heavily dressed to move. He smiled sweetly and attempted to raise his arms when Irene reached down to pick him up.

Back inside, she tried to persuade Barry to eat lunch but nothing tempted him.

'Peanut butter sandwiches?' Nope.

'Toasted sandwiches?' Nope.

'Macaroni?' Nope.

'Eggs?' Nope.

'Soup?' Definitely not. In the end he agreed to eat some cheese. Irene left him sitting at the table mutilating a piece of bright orange Cheddar and took Bobby upstairs for his nap. He'd eaten all his lunch and was sleepy.

They passed that afternoon quietly, ploughing through book after book, colouring, drawing pictures, and, eventually, building a fort. After yet another unsuccessful meal that Barry refused to eat and Bobby accepted gracefully, Irene let them watch television while she had a go at the piano. Bobby wanted to sit near Barry on the sofa and, when Barry would not let him, demonstrating his lack of enthusiasm by bashing Bobby on the head, the baby began to holler. She continued to play 'Summertime' while Bobby screamed. Stopping, Irene tried to console him. Bobby sobbed and looked at Barry who was watching 'Animal Kingdom', unrepentant. None of her efforts to soothe the baby succeeded, including a promise of sweeties, so Irene went back to the piano and played Cole Porter and Irving Berlin, drowning out Bobby's wails.

Later that night, after she had turned off the television and was sitting on the sofa with a book, Irene looked up at the black window. The moose now appeared to be smiling at her. 'Asshole,' she mumbled.

That was the shape her days took; arguments with Barry over food, unsuccessful outings, and Bobby made inconsolable by cruel brotherly acts of Barry's. Irene spent every evening alone with the moose. His eyes looked progressively more moist and alive at the end of each day and, one evening, as she tried to avoid his gaze, she thought she saw him blink. Without looking back at the window she got up and turned off the light. In the dark there was no reflection in the excessively large windows. She sat back down on the settee and stared out at the absolute darkness of the cold Yukon night, wondering what had happened to the aurora borealis.

Once she had sat long enough for her eyes to adjust she discovered that the darkness was not so complete. The moon shone, and in the partial light the landscape was eerily fraught with shadow and movement. Irene thought she could see hundreds of moose moving through the trees, big, angry animals in the frozen peopleless night. She turned the light back on and there he was again, staring at her balefully with just a hint of reproach in his eyes.

Irene did not know a single person within a 1,700 mile radius of where she was staying. She felt trapped in the incomprehensively vast wilderness with two children whom she could not abandon, let alone keep amused. Evading boredom became increasingly difficult. She played the piano more often and louder, cooked elaborate meals that Barry would not eat, and began retiring to bed very early to avoid the eyes of the moose who hung over her life so omnisciently.

On the fourth day Irene decided to take the children and drive into town. As soon as the sun rose she bundled them up and into the truck that had sat in the drive since she arrived. Managing to get it started, she drove into town without any problems. In the shopping centre she felt as if she was seeing adult people for the first time in months. She wanted to sit in one of Whitehorse's many bars, drink herself stupid, and then tell somebody about the moose. But instead, she bought chocolates for the children and headed home.

Irene found the truck large and unwieldy. The front of it stuck out a long way, as did the twelve-foot bed, and the gearstick was almost half her height. As she turned off the main road she began to worry and by the time she was actually at the beginning of the drive to the house she was trembling with fear. Both Barry and Bobby were asleep, satiated with the excitement of their trip into town.

Cautiously, Irene began to drive up the icy, rutted road. Three-quarters of the way there she felt the wheels slip on the frozen troughs and before she knew what was happening the truck escaped her control. It slid violently from left to right and everything she did to stop it made matters worse. After a moment, the duration of an ice age, the truck ceased moving. It was wrapped around a tree next to the house and would not go forward, nor backwards. The children woke up and began to wail. Irene got out of the truck, cursed it, kicked it and the tree, then wept, but the vehicle would not budge.

That night Irene dreamed that the moose spoke to her from his position of honour overhead. 'Are you dumb!' he said gleefully. 'And you thought I looked dumb! I'm going to get you, you know. Just like they got me. There's nobody around for miles. The darkness muffles noise. You're all alone up here, all alone. Nature, and that includes me, is not benevolent up here. It's too big to be kind: too cold.'

Irene backed away from the moose, away from his stare and his threats. But as she moved towards the window the moose came towards her, his disembodied head floating free of the wall. Her back was against the cold glass – she could feel it through her shirt – and then, suddenly, she crashed through it and out on to the snow. When she picked herself up and looked around the house had disappeared. Irene was alone in the Yukon at last, just her and the ghosts of the goldrush.

She woke up in a sweat convinced that the moose in the sitting-room was possessed by some kind of demon.

The same evil spirit inhabited the truck as well – it sat there in the drive waiting for her to put the key back into the ignition so it could take off on another self-destructive run with Irene flailing in front of the dashboard. She lay awake and considered her options. She couldn't live with 1,700 miles of wilderness, not even as an abstract fact. Perhaps, she thought, she should make some kind of offering to appease the moose. Maybe it liked children.

Fingers in the Cookie Jar

When Brenda was a little girl she got into trouble with her best friend's mother once.

'I saw you reach for the biggest bun,' Mrs Benson said to Brenda when she and Debbie came inside and were sitting at the kitchen table.

'What?' asked Brenda, confused.

'I said that I know you reached across the table and took the biggest bun.' Brenda blushed and said nothing. She felt so embarrassed that she couldn't eat or drink and sat in silence while Debbie begged her mother to let her go back outside again. But permission was denied so Brenda went home, mortified.

Still a little girl, Brenda saw her best friend Debbie steal several pennies off the mantelpiece in the sitting-room of a third friend. When Debbie and Brenda left the house Brenda said to Debbie, 'I saw you take those pennies.'

'What pennies?' said Debbie. 'I don't have any pennies. My mum doesn't let me have money. She says I'll spend it on sweets.' Brenda knew that this was probably true. Debbie often had sweets that came from unexplained sources.

When Brenda became a big girl, she left home and moved to the city where she worked in a chain of American restaurants. It was her responsibility to make sure there was a constant supply of thin and over-priced chips which were sold by the ounce. Brenda worked at this job for over two months then one day she was late, the next day she was later, and the next day she got the sack. When she returned home her eldest sister said to her, 'You useless thing you. Can't even hold down a moron's job. Well, I'm tired of having you hang around. You'd better find somewhere else to stay, Brenda. This is the real world you know. You're not a little girl any more.'

So Brenda decided she had to move out of her sister's flat, although she did not have the slightest idea where to go. At the restaurant she had made friends with one other girl who had been sacked about a week before. Brenda remembered where she had put the address and the next day went around to visit Spike.

From the outside, the house was obviously a squat. There were no net curtains at street level and the place had that unmistakable air of dereliction that comes to houses abused and then left to rot by their owners. The guttering along the front eaves hung off at an alarming angle and there were several holes in the roof. Brenda walked up the crumbling staircase to the front door. The bell was broken so she banged as hard as she could. Within a few minutes, the door was pulled open and there, to Brenda's relief, stood Spike.

'Brenda! Hello, how are you? What brings you up this way?' Spike exclaimed, smiling broadly.

'Well . . .' said Brenda, shyly.

'Don't tell me you're still in that hellhole they call a restaurant, are you?'

'No,' replied Brenda, 'I got the sack the other day.'

'Great! You're better off without it. I don't know what I was doing in that dive. All that meat! Yuck!!!'

'I know what you mean,' Brenda said, smiling. 'It was enough to make me a vegetarian.'

'I already was one!' shouted Spike. 'Oh, the horror, the horror! Come in, Brenda, and have a cup of tea.' Brenda followed Spike inside. A few days later she arrived on the doorstep again, this time with all her worldly goods which consisted of an overnight bag and two copies of *La Nausée* by Jean-Paul Sartre. When Spike saw those she said, 'I figure that guy worked in a hamburger bar while he wrote that.' Brenda agreed and was shown to her room.

The house was large with six usable rooms, a kitchen and a bathroom. The toilet was outside in the back garden. The three rooms on the top floor of the house were totally out of bounds due to the holes in the roof. Rain came straight through the ceiling of one room. If you stood in the place where the bucket usually sat and looked up, you could see the sky. In winter the house was heated by several electric bar-fires that were transported from room to room, depending where heat was needed most. There was no gas and no hot water, so meals were cooked and bathwater was heated on the hotplate that sat on top of the disconnected cooker in the kitchen.

When Brenda moved in Spike was living with two other women, one named Vanessa and the other, Martie. None of the young women had jobs.

'Well,' said Spike, 'I've had more shit jobs than a human can stand to have and I'm not going to take it any more.'

Vanessa nodded her head and said, 'When I left school I went on a school leavers' scheme. They put me in an office as a junior. When I realised that I was being paid less than half the wage of the lowest paid person there I left. Nobody is going to make me get them coffee and straighten their ties for money that a dog couldn't live on.'

Martie nodded her head as well and said, 'Since I left school I haven't been able to get a job full stop.' The next day, with instructions from her three friends, Brenda went down to the unemployment office and signed on.

Spike, Martie and Vanessa were all extremely proficient at making a home on less money than a mouse, let alone a dog, could survive on. They drank very little, ate very

little, went out very infrequently, and never bought
clothes, records, or books. At the end of the day they'd go
around to the local market and pick potatoes and leeks
and half-rotten carrots up off the ground and out of the
bins. They were very adept at sorting through rubbish
and salvaging anything usable; the house was furnished
with an eclectic mixture of odd chairs, broken settees, and
pieces of mirror.

Spike had developed a sixth sense when it came to
skips. She could always spot the good ones and her
geographical knowledge of London was defined by what
one could find and where. Covent Garden? Very lucrative
for discarded office equipment, such as files, paper, and
even desks. Pens, paperclips, notebooks: this was where
Spike had found the electric typewriter that she gave
Martie for her birthday, its only fault being a hole where
the '£' key should have been. Soho? Very good for
restaurant rubbish such as mildly damaged chairs, large
empty tins (useful for catching rain as it comes through
the roof), and sometimes even food. Vanessa had once
found an entire box of perfectly good avocados in Soho.
They had eaten guacamole until they were ill.
Hampstead? Now that's the place for furniture, especially beds and settees and dressers and even wardrobes
– the only problem being, of course, that of transport-
ation.

All of this, and more, Brenda learned from her three
companions and before long, with their help, she had
furnished her bedroom.

'The only problem', said Spike one afternoon when it
was raining, 'is jewellery. We can get clothes and even
shoes from the skips and jumble sales, but where can a
girl find a decent pair of ear-rings to wear?'

'Yeah,' said Vanessa, 'I may be on the dole but I don't
want to look like it.'

'That's right,' said Martie, 'ugly. No one should have to
look ugly.'

'Of course,' Spike said, smiling, 'make-up is a problem as well.'

'Mmm,' said the others, nodding.

The next day the four women rose early, got on to their bikes and rode to Oxford Street. They entered one of the many large and undemanding department stores, and, splitting up, wandered in different directions. Martie tried on hats, Vanessa, shoes, Spike, dresses. Brenda watched from a distance, not quite sure of what to do. Looking at stuff she knew she couldn't possibly buy made her nervous: she felt an economic failure, without the power to buy herself a dress.

The three other girls all slowly made their way through the shop, each pausing at different times in front of the make-up and jewellery counters. Brenda watched as they joked with the sales assistants and sprayed themselves with 'J'Accuse' and other perfumes. Then, one by one, they all left by the rear door.

Back at the bikes, Brenda said, 'So, what was that all about?'

They smiled slyly and said, 'Wait and see,' then got on their bikes and rode home. After making a big pot of tea, they sat around the kitchen table emptying their pockets.

'Three lovely pairs of ear-rings. I especially like these large, gold, dangling ones. A bracelet, a pink plastic necklace, and some eyeliner,' said Vanessa.

'A scarf ('ooh, that's nice'), some dark glasses! And a bottle of perfume, worth £35!' announced Martie.

'A matching set of ear-rings, necklace, and bracelet. Toilet water. Lipstick, eyeshadow, BLUSHER! Make-up remover. Bright red nail polish of the non-chip variety. A bow for my hair,' Spike proclaimed.

'Oh!' squealed Martie. 'We'll all be so beautiful! I can't bear it! Let's go again tomorrow!'

'But,' said Brenda, feeling foolish, 'did you steal all of that?'

'Of course,' said Spike, 'or do you think it all just fell into our pockets?'

'But what if you get caught?'

'We don't. We never do. They're too daft.'

That night Brenda lay awake in bed thinking about new clothes and matching accessories. She dreamed about perfume, skirts, hats, and drooled into her pillow. When she woke up the next morning she felt disappointed that her designer dreams weren't true. She walked over to her wardrobe and pulled it open. Her clothes all looked drab, dated and boring. She didn't have any jewellery to speak of, nor any make-up. Life looked dull.

Brenda went downstairs. Vanessa was sitting in the kitchen eating her breakfast and reading a book. 'Where are Spike and Martie?' asked Brenda.

'Oh, they've gone down to the market to get some food. They'll be back very soon I should think.'

'Great,' said Brenda. 'I hope they find some fruit. I'm dying for an orange.'

'Fruit's not so easy to get,' remarked Vanessa. 'It's often bruised or mushy. But sometimes they're lucky, especially Spike. Would you like some tea?'

About an hour later the front door slammed and Martie came running into the kitchen, breathless. 'They've got Spike!' she shouted. 'They picked her up when we weren't watching. They've arrested her and taken her down to the police station! They said it was illegal to take stuff from the bins. They said that even though it was in the bins it was still somebody else's property. The property of the borough rubbish men.'

'Do you mean the police got her?' asked Vanessa, shocked. 'The filth?'

'Yes, that's what I said! They just came along and stopped us. We were going through a big box of peaches that somebody had thrown away. A whole box. It was hardly damaged at all. We tried to talk them out of it, we were polite to them and everything, but it was two female cops and I think they're meaner than the rest of them, they have to be.'

'Well, what are we going to do?' Brenda shouted. 'They've got Spike! We've got to get her out of there!'

'It's no use panicking,' Vanessa said calmly. 'We'll ring Release and get a solicitor. I've got a plan. Martie, you go to the police station and ask to see Spike. I'll go to the phone kiosk and try to get a solicitor to go down to the station. Brenda, you wait here in case Spike gets let out and comes home.'

'All right,' said Brenda, 'I guess there isn't much else that we can do.'

Vanessa and Martie headed off out of the door in a mad rush and suddenly Brenda was left in silence. She sat in the kitchen and wondered what she should do. She put the kettle on to the hotplate and cleaned the teapot of tea leaves. When the kettle boiled, she made tea. Then she sat next to the kitchen window. The sun was streaming in. Everything seemed quite unreal.

A couple of hours later nothing had happened and no one had come home. Brenda was beginning to feel bored and also a little useless. She'd tidied the kitchen, sitting-room, her room, and written a letter to her mum, not mentioning the events of the day. Then she paced about a bit and stood looking out of the sitting-room windows at the street to see if she could spot anyone coming towards the house. But the street was empty. She decided to get on her bike and go and look for the others.

Once outside Brenda felt a little better. She rode around the streets near the house, past where the telephone kiosk stood, but there was no sign of Vanessa. She rode along the High Street and looked in the newsagent's but nobody was in there either. It occurred to her to go to the police station, but then she realised that she didn't know where it was. So she decided to go for a bicycle ride and return home after that.

Before she knew it, Brenda found herself down in

Oxford Street along with the buses and taxis and millions of shoppers. She rode up and down between Marble Arch and Tottenham Court Road several times before tying her bike up outside Selfridges. Entering the large department store through the side doors, she walked up and down the aisles gazing at the perfume, tights and the menswear. She thought to herself, 'I wonder if they've let Spike go yet. I wonder if she'll have to go to jail. Can they really do you for stealing rubbish? I hope she's OK.' Brenda strolled around the ground floor of the store and found herself at the foot of the escalators which carried her up to the first floor, then the second, and then the third: Ladies' Wear and Home Furnishings.

Wandering through the settees and kitchen sets, Brenda began to think about her wardrobe. She needed some new clothes. 'What I need', thought Brenda, 'is a nice dress. That will cheer me up.' She wandered through the racks of clothes and spotted, in amongst the cocktail dresses and the office wear, a lovely red party dress with a wide, round skirt. She went over to the dress and stood looking at it. The price tag said £110.00.

'Hello,' said a woman who had suddenly appeared beside Brenda. 'Can I be of any assistance?'

'This is a nice dress,' Brenda said, 'I'd like to have it.'

'Oh, yes, it's a new style, only been in the shop since yesterday. I think it will be very popular. It comes in other colours, would you prefer it in green or brown?'

'Oh, green I should think, a colour that will give me control.'

'Right, well I'll just go and see if I can find you one. I'll be five minutes.' The woman began to walk away and then paused, turned and said, 'Will that be cash?'

Brenda nodded and smiled. Then she bent over to have a closer look at the dress. It was covered with intricate stitching and looked well made. She took it off the rack and pinned it against her body. It felt cool and light on her skin. She held the dress in her arms carefully and looked down at it tenderly, as if it was a sleeping baby.

'Spike,' she said to the mirror, 'This dress is for you.'

Brenda walked towards the escalator and travelled down the series of moving staircases until she came to the ground floor. Walking past the perfume and the tights, she stopped in front of the electronic anti-shoplifting devices with a vague idea that if the alarm went off she might see Spike sooner than she would otherwise. But nothing happened and Brenda went out of the exit to Oxford Street. She tied the dress on to the back of her bicycle and rode home.

There was still no one there when Brenda arrived back. She carried the dress through the house and into her bedroom then laid it on her bed. It looked lovely and Brenda felt pleased with herself. She sat down to wait for the others to return.

Revolutions Past and Gone

Many years later, Agnes was sorting through her collection of tapes. She had a stack of ancient cassettes with nothing written on them to indicate what they recorded. Agnes picked up a dirty old cassette and plugged it in, expecting to hear some badly muffled Pink Floyd or maybe even the Doors. Instead, when she pushed 'Play' she heard the voice of an old boyfriend, Michel. She'd forgotten that he'd ever made her this tape. He must have been drunk, or on drugs or something, at the time because his thin and reedy young Québécois voice was singing her David Bowie songs, complete with a British accent. A little bit out of tune, a little bit slow, but with a great deal of conviction. Agnes listened while Michel's voice rose out of the tape-machine. It was like hearing the voice of a dead person.

They'd been together back in the heady days, before Quebec felt secure and comfortable, lost the Separatist Movement and elected a Liberal premier. Agnes had lived in Montreal when late at night in the bars in the east of the city everybody was in love with that big romantic idea of Quebec dropping the bossy and boring Anglais and going out on its own. Sceptics said they'd be swallowed immediately by the U.S. but the romantics – the majority – said that it would be wonderful, Quebec would be a

French-Catholic-Socialist State with both divorce and abortion and without censorship laws. The liberating and the sordid all rolled into one.

Those were the days when you could get into a punch-up in Montreal Vieux for being from the wrong province and an inappropriate degree of waspishness could make you a complete social pariah. But even 'les maudits' – the damned – the Anglophones who hadn't left with the exodus of the 1970s, thought that Separatism was sexy, at least as an idea, before one considered the economics of the whole thing.

'We are not to be another Louisiana,' Michel said to Agnes when they first met in a downtown bar. He was trying his best to ignore her; her French was appalling and she was obviously from Alberta or somewhere else similarly Western. But he couldn't simply disregard her like that. She had the most extraordinary eyes and such a nice smile and she obviously wanted to talk to him.

'No, you are not going to be another Louisiana,' Agnes had answered. 'Louisiana is in the U.S. This is Canada you are talking about. We are far too polite to do to you what the Americans did to their French. Besides there are too many of you. And you've got Trudeau. You can't lose now.'

'Trudeau, pah!' snorted Michel. 'He'll sell us down the St Laurent.' Michel decided he really should be ignoring this woman. Who was she anyway, what did she know about Quebec? 'I bet,' said Michel looking at Agnes, 'I bet you are a student at McGill University.'

'How did you know that?' asked Agnes.

'The last frontier of Anglo-Protestant supremacy.'

'That's right. And proud of it.'

At that, Michel got up and took his beer from the table where he'd somehow managed to end up sitting with Agnes. He walked through the smoky bar shaking his head.

Agnes sat at the table watching Michel stomp off. She

looked back down at her beer. She was on her own,
attempting to have a good time away from McGill. The
university was a big disappointment. It was, as Michel
had said, implying it was her fault, a little island of
anglo-culture right in the middle of Montreal, a big,
steamy Québécois city.

But Agnes had come to Quebec because she too had
romantic notions about Separatism. In 1970 when she was
fourteen years old, she was thrilled by Le Fronte de la
Libération du Québec and their revolutionary antics. She
watched everything on the television; it had seemed so
extreme when Trudeau had brought in the army. He was
French, what was he doing? By the time Agnes got to
Quebec Canada's miniature civil war was in the rapidly
receding past and Separatism had become a more accept-
able political issue, fit for the ballot box, not bombs and
guns.

Ten years later, when Agnes heard Michel's voice on
tape it was as though she had pushed a button marked
'Play' in her memory. They had such a good time,
eventually, when Michel got over trying to despise Agnes
and Agnes stopped thinking he was the greatest thing
since Che Guevara. He'd taught her a lot of French and
taken her to places in Montreal that someone so
obviously Western and, well, 'McGill', would never have
known about, let alone ended up in late at night. Agnes
met all kinds of people through Michel, the Greek-
Québécois intellectuals, the Jewish-Québécois intellectuals, the Portuguese-Québécois intellectuals: everybody
was an intellectual in those days. They were all making
films and writing poetry, novels and plays, having parties, doing performances, publishing magazines and
splitting and resplitting into different political factions.
She'd even met Leonard Cohen once, but everybody who
lived in Montreal had met him and no one was allowed to
be the slightest bit impressed.

That first night, in the bar, Agnes had sat by herself for

several hours. She fended off drunks by speaking to them in her bad French, repelling them with her Englishness. She didn't even have to say 'Go away'; they left as soon as they heard her accent. Agnes just sat at her table smoking Gauloises and taking it all in.

Michel had gone off and found his friends who were engaged in a lively argument about, what else, Separatism. They were all shouting and gesticulating and making sweeping generalisations and damning the English in ever more inventive ways. Michel joined in, downing his beer. But he kept finding himself looking across the room at Agnes, sitting there at her table. To him she looked both serene and determined. He could tell she was not about to give up; she wanted to fit in. Eventually Michel surrendered his cool and wandered back over to her table.

'You're still here,' he said.

'Been here for three hundred years,' Agnes answered. 'Ever since we won the war. Don't intend to leave either.' She smiled and Michel was lost.

Agnes continued going to classes at McGill, despite her disillusionment with the institution. She kept thinking maybe she'd run into Marshal McCluhan or Charles Taylor or Hugh McLennan, but of course, that's not the way universities work. She continued struggling with Kant in the library and having arguments with her professors in the Philosophy Department, most of whom were Anglophone, male, middle-aged and pompous, just as Michel imagined them.

'I met the head of department today,' Agnes said one evening when she and Michel had met on Rue St Denis to go drinking with Michel's friends.

'Oh yeah, what was he like?'

'Well, he's a Kierkegaardean Christian Existentialist.'

'Aren't they all?'

'He has devoted his philosophic career to programming a computer that can read all of Kierkegaard and, hopefully, one day when the programme is complete, finish Kierkegaard's "Unfinished Postscript".'

'No.'

'Yes. He even knows Danish. He and Søren, they're like that,' she said holding up crossed fingers.

'Jesus,' said Michel. 'What a place.'

'You should go there with me one day, Michel. Even if it's just to the bar. An insider's view, you know. It would be good for the revolution I'm sure. You can't storm the Bastille without knowing what it's like inside.' Agnes smiled when Michel stuck his tongue out at her.

With each successive school term Agnes moved farther and farther east, away from the university and the student 'ghetto', as the area right next to McGill was called, until eventually she was living with Michel out on East Ontario Est, as the street sign said. They became quite domesticated, speaking French in the evening and English at breakfast, when Agnes couldn't cope with saying 'cornflakes' with Québécois pronunciation. Michel was a student at the Université de Montreal, a whirling pool of radicalism.

As she sat in her sitting-room listening to Michel sing David Bowie songs from ancient history, Agnes asked herself, 'Where is Michel now?'

In the fourth and final year of her degree Agnes had to leave Montreal. Her father died suddenly and her mother was taken ill. She hadn't minded leaving her degree unfinished, from the very beginning it had only been a means for her to stay in Montreal. But she had minded leaving Montreal, of course, and Michel. She felt she had finally penetrated the impenetrable and people were beginning to forget, occasionally, that she was one of the damned.

Neither Michel nor Agnes had expected that Agnes's abrupt departure would end their relationship. That spring they spoke on the telephone regularly, Agnes's voice cracking in French. Michel came to Calgary in the summer to work for a Canadian oil company that needed bilingual employees for negotiations with Quebec. It wasn't his chosen area of interest, but he'd never been West before and was longing to see Agnes. The second day after he arrived they were downtown shopping – Michel needed shirts and ties, items he had never acquired. They stopped in at the liquor store on the way home and Michel bumped into a man who dropped and smashed a bottle of wine. When the enormous Albertan with a red face and a cowboy hat heard Michel's accent as he apologised, the man called him a 'frog-kike-wop' and attempted to punch him in the face. Michel decided he hated cowboys and the West.

A few weeks later the annual Calgary Stampede took place. During the week of festivities, rodeos, fun fairs, parties, horse-races, cattle-roping, and other pseudo-American Wild West antics, Michel and Agnes went to a party. Everybody was shouting 'Yee-hah' and slapping each other on the back and he decided it wasn't such a bad place after all. They spent every weekend camping on the bald prairie. Standing in the middle of a wheat field that seemed to stretch three hundred miles to the endless ridge of the Rockies, he felt he knew Agnes a little better.

The summer ended, Michel went back to Montreal and Agnes's mother's health worsened. When he finished his degree, he found a good job. The referendum took place and the people of Quebec said no to Separatism. Trudeau went in and out, and then in and out again, of retirement. The French language became firmly institutionalised in Quebec through strict legislation. Without warning, years had gone by and Michel was married to somebody else. 'A Québécois girl, no doubt,' Agnes thought as she sat in her sitting-room. 'But I wonder what happened to Michel? I wonder what happened to all the Montreal intellectuals? And what do they argue about now that the urgency of Separatism has faded? Have they stopped making films and writing poetry? Do they still think I'm damned?'

The tape ended and Agnes thought in silence. 'I must go back to Montreal. I must go back and find Michel. I'll go back for La Fête de St Jean-Baptiste. We'll get drunk in the sweaty Montreal night and wander through the streets shouting "Vive Le Québec!" '

Agnes got up, turned the tape-machine off, and went to bed where her husband was already asleep.

The Battersea Power Station

She said out loud to the man conducting the job interview,

'I had to give up my black leather jacket when I realised it had once been animate. I gave it back to its rightful owner, some cow I never met.' And then she said,

'Yeah. We met on the underground. We spent the night snorting cocaine and fucking in the Battersea Power Station.' She continued with, 'No, I don't eat much any more. I kept wondering if it's really fair to eat vegetables. Maybe they have a right to live too. Right now I'm trying hard to work out some way for me to live by photosynthesis. But the sun never seems to shine any more.' Then she smiled and told him her best joke,

'What do you call a man standing in a pot of ratatouille? Basil.' She laughed away to herself. Then, she collected her things and said she had to go home and scare the rats out of the kitchen. She put on her jacket, tearing the lining again, and walked off. She walked through Covent Garden oblivious. She hated it there so she pretended she wasn't there at all. She smiled at the bags of shopping as if they were people and looked at the people as if they were bags of shopping, which some of them actually were. On the Strand she got on a bus. A man sat next to her; it was the man she had met on the underground. He said,

'I quit my job today. My boss underpays me, he fiddles the books, gives people dead turkeys at Christmas, and expects them to be happy. Dead turkeys. I can't believe it. Most people need money.'

'Jobs don't matter anyway,' she said. 'It's a bad thing, doing what you're told to do. You can go on the dole and eat chocolate.'

They got off the bus at the Battersea Power Station and snorted cocaine and fucked all night. When dawn crept through the grimy windows of the control room, he said to her,

'We mustn't snort this stuff, you know. It probably comes from South America or Asia or somewhere and they probably force people to grow it when they should be growing vegetables to eat.'

'Vegetables,' she said. 'Dead turkeys, vegetables, my black leather jacket.'

'You'd look good in a black leather jacket,' he said.

'What do you call a man with a car on his head? Jack.' She said this and sighed and touched the boy from the underground with the back of her hand. 'Maybe photosynthesis is a bad idea, maybe I can survive on sex alone.' So, in the name of scientific experiment, they started to fuck again, while in the boiler room some slime grew, the pigeons cooed, and the girders rusted.

The next day was sunny, so she stretched out on the roof garden and smiled at the sun. With her legs spread-eagled, her arms fully extended, her fingers and toes spread and stretching, her eyes closed, and her gums exposed, she tried very hard to photosynthesise. Just in case she could not live by fucking alone. The sun felt great, all over her body.

After a while one of her flatmates came up on to the garden and said, 'Hey. What are you doing?' She just smiled, exposing her gums a little more. The flatmate said, 'Do you want something to eat?' She shook her head. The flatmate went away. Soon she could smell cooking. She wondered what her flatmate had killed. She got up off the roof, looking hopefully at her arm for a tinge of green, then went down to her room. She fumbled around in the closet for a dress and pulled out a suede jacket instead. Oh no. She sighed to herself, then took it into the sitting-room where her flatmates were devouring things and said,

'Look at this. I'd forgotten all about it. What am I going to do with it, whose is it, does it come from Jersey, Hereford, or Loseley? Some cow I never met.' She smiled at her flatmates and did a brief tap dance. 'What do you call a girl with two eggs, chips, beans, toast, and tea on her head? Caf.' Then she danced away before they could catch her. She walked to the National Film Theatre and watched a Fred Astaire movie. When the lights came on she discovered she was sitting next to the man from the underground. They got on his push-bike, she sat on the seat, he stood and pedalled, and they rode to the Battersea Power Station. From Nine Elms Lane it looms like eternity. Even at night it casts a gothic shadow. He called to her as they rode along, turning his head so the wind would catch his words and carry them to her.

'Being unemployed is like waiting for a train. The train never comes so you amuse yourself by reading the posters backwards. You get to know the posters very well. Soon these posters start to excite you. You are sure they are trying to tell you something, not just about the product, but something about the meaning of life. I'm glad I'm unemployed. It gives me a greater understanding of things.'

'Being unemployed makes me worry about eating,' she said.

Then they were inside the Battersea Power Station, up in the control room, fucking on the parquet floor, reading the dials on the walls when they paused. He said,

'Why do we fuck on the parquet floor?'

'Because the boiler room is too scarey,' she replied.

Then she giggled and said, 'Oh, my suede jacket,' as if those words had meaning, and he said,

'You'd look good in a suede jacket.' Later, when they leaned against the cut-glass windows overlooking the boiler room she said,

'What do you call a man with a pigeon on his head? Cliff. Or Nelson.'

The next day was rainy so she sat in the kitchen and cut up the newspaper and put it back together but with the sentences, paragraphs, articles all mixed up so there was an article on how to holiday in Israel on the overseas news page and an article about the ANC on the entertainment page. One of her flatmates came in and offered to cook her breakfast but she said,

'No, thank you. I am trying to survive on sex alone. Not just ordinary sex, of course, but sex with the man from the underground in the Battersea Power Station. You must understand the connection there. Sex – energy – power – fuel – electricity – you know, all those things. Sex in the Battersea Power Station, that should be enough, don't you think?' Then she put on her favourite dress and walked to the British Museum. Peering into a mummy case she saw the face of the boy from the underground. She turned around and he was there. He took her in his arms and they did a slow waltz through the room full of large, wonderful, Egyptian things, past the art deco porcelain and into the room with the sixteenth-century religious icons. They zigzagged through history like a sewing machine and came to rest in front of Oscar Wilde's handwritten manuscript of *The Importance of Being Earnest* and she cried to the museum guard who stood watching,

'We will go down in histrionics,' then she laughed and they salsaed all the way to the Battersea Power Station and fucked on the floor of the boiler room. They looked up at the decaying girders and columns, they listened to the pigeons cooing, and the water that ran along the floor

collected in a pool around them. His voice echoed through
the enormous chamber when he said,

'Being with you is like being with a spirit. Being with
you is like just catching a train. Being with you is like
riding downhill,' and she said,

'Thanks, I like you too. You always show up at the right
time.' They kissed for a while and the Battersea Power
Station groaned from disuse. Then she said,

'What do you call a man with a bog on his head? Pete.'
They laughed and then after a while he said,

'That's my name.'

So We Swing

A great many physically astounding feats can be performed on a set of playground swings. You can rock from side to side slowly, jerk back and forth quickly or even smash into the person on the next swing. We used to have swing wars when we were very young, screaming out of the sky as we pushed ourselves off, braced for the crash. We'd twist the seat around and around until the chains were wound up tight and high, lifting us far off the ground. Then we'd let go and the chains would unwind, spinning our bodies so quickly that once it was over we'd have to get off and stamp our feet on the firm and, thankfully, solid earth.

One favourite game was to stand up on the seat and swing at such an angle that the playground would disappear completely, leaving only the sky. It was almost as if we could fly. The dare-devils could jump off mid-swing, hurtling to the ground like giggling bombs, but I would always end up dragging my feet in order to slow down.

As I walked by the swings tonight I heard a small girl chanting at a small boy, 'I'm not your friend, I'm not your friend.'

'I don't care,' replied the boy.

'Neither do I . . .' said the small girl, pausing, 'I'm going to die soon anyway.'

133

I walked on and left them to quarrel, wondering how the notion of death had reached such a small girl so young. Perhaps she was making childish threats or maybe she had foreseen something that we, the big people, had missed. The question I asked myself then was this: how will she die? There are so many ways, like the junkies next door, or the homeless alcoholics on the corner, or those who make their suicide more sudden and real, off a block of flats or a bridge. Or perhaps this small girl will die a daredevil's death and leap as the swing reaches the highest point in its arc. She will throw her feet out first, her body following after, and she will smash herself into a small girl pile of death on the very pavement we all at one point have feared smashing our own heads on.

I had a friend in school who conducted the preliminary stages of all her major adolescent romances on the set of swings behind the primary school. On warm summer evenings this friend of mine would lead her prospective boyfriend to the swings and there they would sit talking and showing off to each other. There is something re-markably sensual about flying through the warm soft night air with your legs stretched out in front. Swinging in counter-rhythm you swish by the boy you like: behind, in front, behind, never quite touching.

It always worked, this swing business. The boys my friend took to the swings always fell in love with her. Sometimes even now I long to get on the swings myself, just to fly through the air like a child.

But my friend is gone now, she probably married one of those boys, and the childhood swinging sessions have been replaced by other, more adult, thrills and chills. Now when I walk past the playground on my way to the bar I rarely glance over at the wooden seats or notice their slightly macabre chains hanging in the moonlight.

Last night I was disappointed to see Lisa kissing the pushy boy who hangs out in the speakeasy. Every weekend I watch as he gets drunk and falls over. When I left the bar early this morning, they were asleep in a pile on the floor. Nick wasn't there so I assume that in her boredom she let that pushy boy prey upon her. Lisa has been chasing Nick for over half a year now. His expression when he greets her always seems to be saying, 'Go ahead, get on with it,' and Lisa does, full force. She turns her whole body on to Nick, her face saying, 'I want you, I want you,' her hands saying, 'I want you, I want you,' she herself probably saying, 'I want you, I want you,' into his ear, her lips touching his neck. He lets her do it, he leans back in his chair as she throws herself at him, recklessly hurling her body across the room.

The rooms in the speakeasy are dark, lit only by fire or candle light but when Lisa walks into a room she can sense immediately if Nick is there. She told me this, but if you watch it's obvious. She walks into the room with her shoulders held very high, as if she is sniffing the air. She always looks tense and when she spots Nick her body tightens; if he isn't around her body crumples with disappointment.

Most nights, Lisa stands at the bar and talks to someone else. When Nick is sitting at a table with his friends Lisa keeps a smile on her face but every few minutes she loses track of the conversation. Her head turns Nick's way and she has a quick look, just to see if he's still there, or better yet, to catch him looking at her. Then she turns back to whichever pushy boy is occupying her and smiles and nods.

I sit in the corner in the dark room, drinking the cheap red wine that they sell there, and watch as every few moments Lisa looks at Nick. To me, her eyes are singing that refrain of 'I want you, I want you' and I know she feels desperate, her body is full of desire, she is making herself feel dizzy. The openness of her hunger startles me and seems wonderful.

One night, several months ago, Lisa walked in and found neither Nick nor any of those pushy boys that she

is always falling back on. She looked a little tired, as do
most of us who frequent the speakeasy. She asked the
bloke behind the counter for a bottle of wine, then came
and sat at my table. We knew each other through con-
tinual sightings at the bar; we probably wouldn't have
spoken had we passed in the street. But there was nobody
else for her to talk to on that night. Besides, she must have
seen me talking to Nick on previous nights and this
formed a connection in her mind.

'Do you mind if I sit here?' she asked. I replied by
pulling a chair over for her. 'None of my friends seem to
be here tonight. That's unusual,' she said, looking
around. 'I almost always know somebody. I wonder
where they all are? Have you got any ideas?' I decided to
be blunt and told her that Nick had gone away for the
weekend.

'Oh?' she replied, blushing. 'He didn't say anything
about that. Although I suppose that shouldn't surprise
me.' She paused and drained her glass. 'We haven't been
on the best of terms lately.' I had heard from friends Nick
and I had in common that they'd never been on particularly good terms. Nick had a girlfriend somewhere, Indo-
nesia, I think. She was an artist and they didn't see each
other often but that was where Nick's attentions were
directed, as far as I knew.

'He's a wonderful person really, Nick, don't you think?'
Lisa said, expecting me to agree. I smiled and nodded
without saying that I thought he was just all right.

'Don't you think he's incredibly good-looking?' Thinking about all lanky six feet four inches of Nick and his
cheekbones I had to admit she had a point, but I didn't tell
her that the most interesting thing about him was her
obsession with him.

Lisa drained another glass of wine. She was drinking
quickly and mercilessly, as usual. 'We had an affair, did
you know that?' I shook my head. 'Yeah, well we did. I
think he is so beautiful. We had an affair, but he doesn't

seem to want to see me all that much any more. I still want to see him though. That's why I come to this place, to see him. I don't really like places like this, no offence. But it doesn't always work out the way I want.' I was surprised by her frankness. I poured her another glass of wine.

'I feel pretty bad about it. I thought he was beautiful the first time I met him, but that was almost a year ago. He's a friend of some friends. We met here. Doesn't everybody?' she said, giggling. 'I shouldn't say that he's handsome too often because he is charming and intelligent and interesting as well but for some reason when I think of him it is his looks that I think of first. We talked to each other a bit, he winked at me a few times. Then one night it was very late. Everyone was going home and somehow I managed to talk myself into asking him to come home with me and he did. He did.' Lisa smiled broadly at me. 'It was great. I didn't believe that he would actually stay until he had all his clothes off and was kissing me in my bed, under my blankets. But he did. And the next night as well. And then the next weekend . . . well, it was too good to be true. Beautiful men don't just fall from the sky like that.'

Lisa stopped talking for a moment and poured herself another glass of wine, offering me some which I accepted. There was more than one drunkard in this place. Then she spoke again. 'I have this problem. I fall in love with men I think are beautiful and they always turn out to be unobtainable. Oh, sometimes they let you get them into bed but that doesn't mean very much somehow. There's something in the beauty that is unobtainable.' Lisa paused and I thought to myself that it was more likely to be the other way around – there is something about the unobtainable that is beautiful – a well-known principle of consumer culture.

'Sometimes I think I took advantage of him by seizing him at a moment when he didn't particularly care what he did. Or maybe he took advantage of me, letting me do all the hard work, make the decisions. I asked him one day why he'd slept with me, since he didn't seem so keen to do it again. He said that it seemed like a good idea at the time and there wasn't anything else to do, so why not? I don't think that's very nice. It meant such a lot to me. I told him so.'

'You know what he told me then?' she asked, looking at me without waiting for me to reply. 'That he doesn't find me sexually attractive. That he likes me but he's not attracted to me. Then he said that it had nothing to do with me, it was all his problem, but I don't know what he meant by that. If I was thinner and darker he'd probably change his mind. Other men think I'm sexually attractive. He made it sound like he only fucked girls who look like they stepped out of adverts. At first I thought how it must be awful to be so shallow and physical but then I realised that I always think of Nick's looks first. He must be pretty arrogant to imagine that I like him for something that includes his mind and his heart as well as his body when, really, I don't know him at all. He's just this friend of some friends.'

Lisa didn't look at me when she finished but looked out across the room, as if she thought Nick might have walked in and overheard her. 'That's not it as far as I'm concerned though,' she said shaking her head. 'I think he'll change his mind if I persist for long enough. I'll beat him down with my devotion. It can be done, you know,' she said, looking at me angrily. 'I've seen it done. We're friends now. I swallow my lust, drown it with lager and wine and won't sit too near to him. If I do there's always the chance that I'll stand up and beat my breast and shout at him, "I am sexually attractive you fool, the most sexually attractive person around and you are really stupid if you don't see that." ' She paused, 'I wish he wasn't so handsome.'

Well, as I said, that was several months ago and when I saw Lisa in the speakeasy the next weekend she was there at the bar still stealing looks at Nick. He ignored her but she didn't speak to me again. Either she'd forgotten our conversation or I was incidental to her thought processes. I continued to watch her.

There was a night not very long ago when I was coming home late. As I walked past the playground I could see Lisa there with a few of her pushy boyfriends. She was on the swings laughing and swinging up into the warm night air, flying very high, her legs stretched out ahead of her. Each time she reached the highest point in her arc she would turn her head quickly and look at Nick's window across the playground. Is he there, can he hear me, does he know I'm here? Will he come and swing with me? In those quick glances before the swing came down once again, in that brief flash of Lisa's eyes, there seemed a greater declaration of love than any words or endless paeans could express. She looked, at once, desperately unhappy and full of passion and, somehow, to me that seemed wonderful.

I walked by and Lisa kept on swinging. Sometimes she must think she is flying. It's almost as though she is keeping herself up in the air with will-power alone. If Nick had come out to the playground to see her right then I'm sure she would have leapt off mid-swing and flown through the air into his arms. And I'd admire her for it, even if he dropped her or she missed him and smashed her head open on the solid earth below.

The Flat-Sitter

One day the hitherto benevolent local authority, particularly vulnerable to squatters with its massive surplus of derelict property and lack of funds, suddenly awoke and, with a roar, swiped Stella's house off the face of the earth. It was as though a slumbering bear had been aroused by a bumble bee. Stella had buzzed happily and innocently in her little house for too long.

Since then, chance, luck, or the rising salaries of her friends had enabled Stella to avoid homelessness through serial flat-sitting. Her friends felt more secure, as they lay in the sun in Ibiza or Sri Lanka, knowing that someone responsible was keeping the burglars away.

Stella's first engagement had come about when Sally and Zoë went off to Greece for ten days; Stella moved in with explicit instructions on which plants liked water and which did not. For the first few days alone in Sally and Zoë's flat, Stella was cautious and polite, behaving as though she were a house guest whose hosts were only momentarily absent. She slept in the spare room, keeping her toothbrush in her make-up bag which in turn she kept in her suitcase. She watered the to-be-watered plants and washed the dishes immediately after every meal. When Sally and Zoë returned they pronounced her a model flat-sitter and took her out to dinner in a posh

141

restaurant. It was on the success of those first ten days that Stella's reputation as dependable was founded.

Shortly after that, Stella moved into Stan and Matthew's flat for a fortnight. Stan and Matthew were going to Barcelona and they left Stella on her own in their big old house that stood just across the road from a park. Once they'd explained the cooker and left, Stella began to feel a bit more expansive than she had in the previous flat. She moved into Stan and Matthew's own bedroom, began leaving the breakfast dishes in the sink all day, read a letter from Stan's mother that she found on top of the television late one night and towards the end of the fortnight went out in the evening wearing Matthew's aftershave cologne.

'You smell great tonight Stel,' her friend had said lecherously. Stella smiled.

Still, she refrained from dipping into Stan and Matthew's collection of twelve-year-old whisky and did not scratch any of their records. Her reputation remained intact.

Stella's life went on and she moved from one flat-sitting engagement to the next. During the daytime she worked in a sandwich bar doing everything from the accounts to making egg mayonnaise. The job was rather poorly paid but Stella liked it. She had a certain amount of control. Conquering the lunchtime queue made her feel happy. In the evenings she went out with those of her friends who were not on holiday and after that she went home to someone else's flat. She became quite accustomed to a lifestyle of shifting and strangeness.

Still, when Bev and Joe asked Stella to stay in their flat while they were in India she felt relieved.

'Two months!' she shouted at Bev. 'Two whole months! You don't know how happy this makes me!'

'Oh,' said Bev, 'well if I knew how badly you wanted to get rid of us we would have gone sooner.'

'Please, don't get the wrong idea!' said Stella, still

shouting. 'I love you both dearly and if you don't come back I'll miss you terribly, but, two months, it's too good to be true.'

So Stella ensconced herself at Bev and Joe's. By this time her flat-sitting technique had advanced to a record level of casualness. Simply by taking a quick stroll around a new flat Stella found she became intimate with it immediately. She had been to Bev and Joe's before, for dinner and parties, but there are always certain aspects to a home that the infrequent visitor misses. For example, until the evening after Bev and Joe's departure, Stella had not known about their large collection of Bruce Lee videos. Nor had she suspected that when they were not cooking lobster bisque and bulghar wheat salads for their dinner guests, they dined on enormous quantities of frozen potato chips and fish fingers. And, if asked prior to moving in, Stella would never have guessed that behind the Miles Davis records Bev and Joe had Tammy Wynette and Loretta Lynn, and that underneath the biographies of Rosa Luxembourg they kept Jackie Collins and Barbara Cartland.

But Stella took all these revelations in her by now professionally adaptable stride and only blushed slightly when she discovered the oddly textured and shaped sex toys in the drawer beside the bed.

'I am here for the duration,' Stella said out loud, dropping an unusual green object back into the drawer. Other people's intimacies did not affect her.

Bev and Joe's flat was simple – two bedrooms, one of which was used as a study/guest room, a kitchen with a table in it, a sitting-room, and a decent-sized bathroom. Although fairly cluttered, it was comfortable and posed no problems to Stella in her role as flat-sitter. Not even the plants were complicated. At night a bright street-lamp shone orange through the bedroom window but Stella quickly grew to appreciate it. When she was watching television in bed she did not have to get up and turn on

the light in order to find out what the newspaper said was
on next.

Stella had never before watched television in bed – it
seemed a strangely American habit to her – but while she
was staying at Bev and Joe's she suddenly took to it like a
duck to water. On the third night that she was at home on
her own she sat up with a huge plateful of thawed and
fried potato chips and watched her first ever Bruce Lee
video. Stella imagined that this was exactly what Bev and
Joe did on their nights in together. She fell asleep with a
can of beer in her hand just as Bruce was about to make
his three hundredth kill.

Watching Kung-Fu in bed while eating lovely greasy
chips was not the only habit that Stella unintentionally
adopted when she moved into Bev and Joe's flat. She
continually found herself doing things that she felt sure
the occupiers did themselves. In the mornings she got up
and ate cornflakes in her underwear. She began drinking
her coffee black and did not pick the dirty clothes up off
the floor for days. During the second week in the flat she
left unsigned cheques for both the milkman and the
paper-boy and the following Sunday morning she found
herself playing a Johnny Cash album at the wrong speed
with the vague hope of annoying someone although she
was not sure who.

During the day Stella went to work and behaved as she
had done for several years. Nothing unusual, new or
different took her fancy there.

By the third week when Stella came home from work
she found herself feeling inexplicably cross as soon as she
stepped inside the door of the flat. On Thursday evening
when she opened the front door and stepped inside she
felt an absolute fury burst forth. Slamming the door shut,
she stomped into the sitting-room, dumped her things in
a pile, turned on both the radio and the television as
loudly as possible and threw herself down on the couch.
After several minutes she realised she was waiting for

someone to come into the room and start fighting with her. Looking down at her hands she saw she was clenching her fists and her knuckles had turned white. Stella stood up and shook herself violently, once, and then again. She walked around the sitting-room, turned the television off and the radio down. Then she went into the kitchen and poured herself a drink.

The next morning she got up and, after the now familiar cornflakes and underwear routine, went off to work. She felt perfectly normal all day and had an enjoyable evening out with friends. Having had quite a lot to drink, she was extremely sleepy on the underground on the way home. But as soon as she got through the front door of the flat she felt an uncontrollable rage well up inside her again. She hurled her coat to the floor and, quite without planning it, shouted, 'I hate you! I hate you when you come home like this! You make me want to crawl with disgust. Why do you do it? Why?'

'Because,' Stella replied to herself, 'because you're so bloody boring and self-righteous and proper, that's why! You and your godforsaken family.' She walked over to the record-player and put the Johnny Cash LP on at 45 rpm again.

'Don't do that to my Johnny Cash records! You are so mean and horrible! You know that record means a lot to me. Christ, take it off!!' Stella marched around the room a bit and found herself struggling near the stereo. 'Leave it,' she shouted, 'I like it better this way.'

'You only do it because you know I hate it!' Stella shouted, then she ran down the hallway and locked herself in the bathroom and turned on the shower full blast. When she got out and dried herself off the music had stopped and shortly after that she was in bed with a plate of chips watching Bruce Lee.

The next morning Stella ran into the occupant of the flat downstairs on the pavement outside the door of the building. Bev had introduced them prior to her departure.

'So,' said the neighbour, 'Bev and Joe back early, are they?'

'Umm,' said Stella slowly, puzzled. 'No, they're not due back for another six weeks or so.'

'Oh,' said the neighbour, frowning, 'that's odd. I could have sworn I heard them last night.' The neighbour then blushed.

'That must have been me,' replied Stella quickly. 'I have a difficult time with the record-player. It's a bit more technologically advanced than I am.'

'Oh,' said the neighbour, still looking confused.

'Bye,' Stella said walking away. She went home to stay with her parents for the weekend and did not return to the flat until late Monday night. She managed to get into bed without any incidents and just before she went to sleep wondered if she had dreamed the whole thing.

The week passed uneventfully and Stella went out to a party on Friday evening. At the party she drank rather a lot of beer and smoked a fair amount of dope. A friend dropped her back at Bev and Joe's in his car and by the time she got through the front door of the flat she was speeding with anger.

'You are so fucking late, where the fuck have you been?' she shouted.

'None of your goddamned business!' she shouted back.

'You've been out with that person again, haven't you? Ugh, I can smell it, I can smell it on you. You are disgusting,' Stella said very slowly, her lip curling. 'You make me feel sick.'

'I make you sick? Well you make me fucking well feel like goddamned dying, that's how you make me feel. Every night on my way here I realise how much I hate you. You and this godforsaken filthy flat.' Stella stormed over to the record-player, snatched Johnny Cash off the turntable, held it up above her head and then quickly brought it down across her raised knee. The record broke cleanly in half. 'Take that, you bastard!' she shouted.

'You broke it, you fucking broke it, goddamn you!' Clutching her hair and gritting her teeth she muttered, 'I'll teach you to break my records,' then she marched out of the sitting-room and into the bedroom and over to the bedside table. She pulled the top drawer all the way out of the table on to the bed.

'No, no,' she shouted, standing back away from the bed a bit. 'Not the sex toys,' she said deploringly, 'not my collection.'

'Your collection makes me feel ill, you pervert.'

'You never said that before, hypocrite!'

'I never realised what a pig you are before.'

Stella picked up the drawer full of strange little gadgets and went to the window. After a brief struggle she opened it, and, before she could shout anything else, emptied the drawer into the street below. Without saying another word, she picked up her keys and her coat and her cheque book and walked out of the flat, slamming the door.

Outside on the pavement Stella stood waiting for a cab to go by. She examined the things that lay strewn across the ground. It was an odd assortment of what looked like over-sized rubber jumping jacks, tiny plastic dildoes, and things that resembled mutant rubber ducks. She kicked one of them across the street just as she saw a cab approaching.

When she arrived at Sally and Zoë's, they were about to go to bed having also been at the party.

'Stella!' said Sally looking surprised. 'What are you doing here this time of night? Have you locked yourself out of Bev and Joe's?'

'No,' said Stella. 'Listen, Sal, do you know if Bev and Joe argue a lot?'

A Mother's Advice

Before Graham died Lucille had not thought it possible that she would find herself turning into her mother. She always knew that there might be little things she could not avoid, like the lines around her eyes and the slight propensity towards cuddliness that made her start when she looked at herself in the mirror after a particularly heavy night. Lucille thought she could gauge her judgment by measuring her own responses against what she guessed would be her mother's. This parent curled her lip at bad house-keeping so Lucille embraced filth; her mother was warm and comforting so Lucille tried to stay hard and unyielding. As she grew older these uncompromising stands sometimes made her feel tired but one look at the mirror in the morning, the time she resembled her mother most obviously, never failed to smarten her up.

Before Graham died Lucille felt steadfast in her absolute hatred of couples. Since discovering sex at the tender age of fourteen, she had made it clear to her multitude of lovers that not one of them was allowed to lay any claim on her. Not only did she shun marriage and all common-law arrangements, she assiduously avoided seeing less than two men at a time. She would rather be celibate than 'in a relationship' and would throw any poor fool out of her bed if he whispered words vaguely related to fidelity. Lucille never bothered about missing any of the men she chucked out – there were always at least two replacements.

That was before Graham died.

When Graham fell ill Lucille felt ill in sympathy. They were friends, the two of them. After meeting in an exercise class, they spent many an evening sodden with drink and caked with dried sweat, gloating over their latest conquests. If Lucille liked lots of men, so did Graham, and they had a kind of sexual empathy not uncommon between gay men and heterosexual women. Her mother would never have understood.

When the first warning signals came Lucille ignored them and when Graham worsened she ignored that as well. It was as though she gave him the odd evening's respite. Graham seemed to appreciate it; Lucille knew he had other friends who were there to help with the reality. When their visits began to take place in the hospital she and Graham pretended they were elsewhere and Lucille became religiously jolly. She would have been incapable of behaving any other way, even if he'd requested it.

On her last visit Graham was not quite capable of jolliness and Lucille fled in tears. Then he died and she was left on her own wondering what he expected her to do now. In an attempt to recover, she took a fortnight off from work and flew to Spain for a holiday. As she had booked into a cheap package deal for single people, something that, despite her predilection for bed-hopping, she'd never done before, she took off expecting to spend the time 'fucking herself silly'.

But in her bikini on the Costa Brava beach Lucille found herself fending off advances. The first couple of nights she sat alone in her hotel room, explaining to herself that she needed a few days to think about Graham and relax. So she worked on her tan and said no to the many offers of drinks.

On the third day she came off the beach in the late afternoon and sat in the shade of a bar.

'Now look here,' she said to herself, 'stop being such a stick-in-the-mud. Graham wouldn't have wanted this. What's slowing me down? I don't want to spend this fortnight alone, do I?'

That was when she spotted him, across the road on the miniature golf course. He seemed to be practising putting on his own. Lucille watched as he swung his club carefully and then gave a small jump of victory when the ball went into the hole. His concentration was admirable, as was his tan. After seeing him putt an endless string of holes-in-one, Lucille picked up her towel and walked across the street to the fence beyond which he played.

'Hello,' she called out, assuming he was English. 'Not bad, for an amateur.'

He straightened his back and looked up at her, smiling. 'Hello,' he said, 'do you want to play?'

'No,' said Lucille, 'I don't do things in miniature. I prefer them big, you know, life-size,' then she smiled at her own suggestiveness. She found it was a tactic that always disarmed and sometimes charmed. 'Want to have a drink?'

'OK,' he said, 'I'll just finish this round.' Moments later Lucille found herself confronted with the product of her wiles.

'Well,' she said, 'what are you doing in Spain?'

'Escaping Britain, I think. How about you?'

'Escaping Britain, my job, my friends, my family, you know, the works.'

'That sounds rather extreme. What prompted that?'

'A death,' Lucille answered, regretting it immediately.

'Oh, I'm sorry to hear that. Was it someone close?'

'Unbearably,' said Lucille, then she smiled and changed the subject. Within an hour they were in her hotel room and she heard herself saying, 'Just a moment, I'd like to have a quick shower, I'm very oily from the beach.' She left him lying on the bed, his baggy shorts pulled taut in anticipation.

Under a stream of hot water Lucille lathered her body which glistened with health and sunshine. She surveyed her flat stomach, her strong legs, her brown hands, and she found herself thinking of Graham. He had become unimaginably wasted and grey while he died, utterly unlike the person who had shared her obsession with looks. Lucille thought about the man in the other room and how Graham would have hooted in appreciation of his body when she described it. Then she realised that she could not remember, or perhaps did not know, the man's name. She stuck her wet head between the shower curtains and shouted, 'Hey, what did you say your name was?'

'Graham,' came the reply.

'Oh Jesus,' thought Lucille, 'I wish I'd never asked.' She stuck her head back under the shower and scrubbed her body with renewed vigour.

Lucille's mother had married young and expected her daughter to do the same. Throughout her girlhood Lucille had had advice dispensed to her from the kitchen sink. The washing-up seemed to make her mother philosophical.

'Lucille,' she would say, 'men like their wives fresh and neat and pure. Young women seem so quick to hop into bed with every dumb sod who comes along these days – it can only be bad news. You lose your self-esteem as well as your reputation Lucille, they love you and then leave you with nothing. What you want is a good man who'll take care of you.'

Lucille would continue drying the dishes. At the age of eight she listened closely to her mother; she listened quite carefully at nine as well. At ten she half-listened, just in case anything new was said. She tried to get her mum to talk about sex when she was eleven but all she heard was some mumbo-jumbo about marriage and babies, and so by the time she was twelve she stopped listening altogether. By the age of sixteen she was more sexually experienced than her mother would ever be. Promiscuity brought Lucille release from a life she thought was otherwise mundane.

Eventually she came out of the shower wrapped in towels and went back into the bedroom where Graham was lying in the same position, as handsome, available and excited as ever.

'Sorry I took so long but baby oil makes dirt really stick to my body,' she said, by way of an excuse.

'That's OK,' he said, 'I don't mind waiting.' He smiled and asked, 'Where do you keep that baby oil?' and Lucille felt herself melting back into her old routine. 'Keep sinning,' was what she used to say to Graham when they parted, 'Keep sinning and keep your pecker up.' It never failed to make him laugh.

Lucille dropped her towels and lay down on the bed beside Graham and, although she could not bring herself to call him by name, she proceeded to become intimate with his body. He seemed to want to lick every conceivable part of her so she lay on her back and stared into space.

He had not asked about birth control – but they never did. The assumption was that a woman so intent on having sex with complete strangers would have taken care of that. They were, of course, correct. As always, her body responded famously but her mind wandered far away from the slightly seedy Costa Brava hotel room. She stared out of the window at the neon sign. 'Octopussy Disco' flashed over and over again.

Lucille remembered how before Graham had become seriously ill he had spent a couple of months being angry. Once when they met he said to her, 'I never thought it would happen to me, I mean, I'm just too much of a golden boy for this. Too brassy, too fast, too strong. I always thought it was just another part of the great

right-wing conspiracy, you know, like the weather and
unemployment. They wanted us to give up and come
home, to stop having so much fun. I thought it was just a
threat, the kind my mother would have used to make me
behave.' At the time Lucille had nodded and poured
Graham another drink. They had both taken great pleasure in such defiance of the doctor's advice. Until Graham
realised he was going to die he had gone out of his way to
be naughty, although he had managed to give up sex
pretty quickly. 'I'm not that thick-skinned,' he'd said to
Lucille during one of his weaker moments.

Lucille's thoughts were interrupted by the other Graham. 'Do you mind if I pour some more of this oil on your
body?' he asked.

'No,' said Lucille absently, as if he'd requested another
slice of cake. 'Go right ahead.'

Graham had never offered Lucille any advice or become
at all sentimental during his decline. He had never said,
'If this can happen to me it can happen to you,' although
from time to time when she had tried to entertain him
with stories about her social life she thought that she
spotted a shadow of admonishment in his eyes. The fact
was that while Graham was dying Lucille started seeing
even more men. She felt as though she had to do it for
Graham as well as herself, to prove to them both that it
was not the sex that was killing him, it was something
else. Having always thought of herself as way ahead of the
crowd, she could not quite believe that promiscuity had
so quickly become a thing of the past. 'Still plenty of
victims around to be had,' she said to him with bleak
irony.

But Graham did not say anything to Lucille; it would
have broken their unspoken pact, although she now
found herself wishing he had. He had probably thought
that she would accuse him of turning into her mother, but
she would not. Her mother had told her, repeatedly, that
pre-marital sex would lead to grief, but the threat it held

for her mother was very different from that now threaten-
ing Lucille.

'I always thought my greatest fear was the nuclear
bomb,' Graham had said. 'I never thought I'd become a
sort of nuclear bomb of my own.' Lucille had laughed
loudly when he'd said that, and a nurse had popped her
head through the door disapprovingly. Graham had
laughed as well but when they stopped their expressions
were grim.

'You're not a nuclear bomb,' said Lucille. 'You're just
ill.'

Once again, the stranger forced Lucille away from her
thoughts. He had climbed on top of her and was sliding
around in the oil spread all over her body, attempting to
push his way between her legs. Lucille held them
clamped together, almost instinctively.

'Hey,' said Graham, 'What are you doing?'

'Oh nothing,' said Lucille, relaxing. 'I was just thinking
about my mother.'

'Your mother?' he said, breathing heavily.

'Yes,' she said slowly, 'my mother thinks it's the wrath
of God and that we had it coming to us. A girl's got to
keep her reputation intact or God only knows what will
become of her. Mother will be able to say that she told us
so, she knew it would happen all along. But mother,' said
Lucille, pausing, 'she got it all wrong.'

'What are you talking about?' Graham whispered in
Lucille's ear.

'Morality,' replied Lucille, 'my mother's ill advice.'

A Curious Dream of Entrapment

Hilda was a feminist, one of the tough kind who will not take no for an answer and is able to growl at men when they get in her way. She set standards for herself that her suffragette grandmother would have admired, had she lived to see what form The Movement had taken. Hilda was tall and slender and had dark wavy hair and large, dark brown eyes that flashed when certain topics were mentioned. She wore short skirts, flat shoes, and carried a large handbag full of an assortment of papers and notebooks that could take her half an hour to sort through at meetings. Most people who knew her would agree that Hilda was impressive.

Tony was Hilda's boyfriend. Like both his parents, his grandparents, and their parents before them, Tony belonged to the Communist Party of Great Britain. Every year he had been sent to a summer camp on the Baltic Sea where he had been taught Russian and how to drink vodka. Hilda's feminism posed little problem for Comrade Tony and his family of communists, in fact he wouldn't have had it any other way. Hilda could have considered herself lucky, as many of her friends did, but she did not.

Tony and Hilda lived in a flat which they owned in Muswell Hill, a suburb in North London. Every Wednesday night they both attended meetings – Hilda went to her Feminist Society and Tony to his branch of the CPGB. These groups both met above pubs and a large part of each meeting was allotted to time for the members to vent their frustrations with regard to modern-day society's lack of both feminist and communist elements. This time proved invaluable to all the members concerned and especially to Hilda and Tony who often felt very frustrated and oppressed by the world in which we live. Hilda could not bear to be treated like a numbskull and hooted at by men, events that took place regularly. Tony could not bear capitalist culture full stop. So at their meetings they would both drink and shout a fair amount and then return to their flat, feeling greatly relieved.

Back at home whoever arrived first began to cook a modest meal which the two of them ate, seated on the floor and accompanied by a bottle of wine and some soothing music. If it was winter they had an open fire – in summer, an open window. The food and the wine seemed wonderful to the two relaxed companions as they discussed their respective meetings and told each other all their news. Eventually Hilda and Tony would push aside the plates and end up, there, on the floor, in front of the window or the fire, making love. There was something about Communism and Feminism that made them both incredibly horny. Neither of them knew why.

After such an evening, having had rather more to drink than usual, Hilda had a long and complicated dream. She was running away from something that alternated, as things are prone to do in dreams, between being three separate items: Tony; a large disembodied penis; and Nick, a previous boyfriend. She was terrified and ran as fast as she could. Eventually Hilda began to weaken as the thing in pursuit became an invisible force. She ran slower and slower until, finally, she stood still. The moment she stopped a vine began to sprout from the earth below her. This vine grew up Hilda's legs, it curved around her torso and sprouted extra branches which grasped her arms as well. She watched with horror as it grew and then she awoke in a sweat.

Hilda sat up in bed. Tony slept on, undoubtedly dreaming of a Utopia somewhere, as she walked into the kitchen to make herself a cup of tea. She perched on one of their high stools beside the fridge and tried not to think about the dream. Getting out one of the many cookbooks which were propped up by the coffee machine, Hilda began to bake a cake. She mixed together a huge amount of eggs and milk and sugar, fluffy and light like spun syrup and, at about four, popped several cake tins into the oven. Then she went into the other room and read until the timer buzzed and she could pull the cakes out. They fell from their tins like ripe fruit from a tree and Hilda went back to her novel while they cooled. It was just getting light when she began to cut them into shapes and put on the icing.

When Tony got up at eight o'clock he found Hilda in the kitchen putting the finishing touches on what looked very much like a cake-baby.

'Hilda?' he said, 'Whatever are you doing sweetheart?'

'Good morning Tony,' said Hilda, 'I've made us a cake.'

'But have you been up all night?'

'I suppose I have. I had a horrible dream and I couldn't sleep, so I got up and decided to make a cake.'

'But darling, you so rarely make cakes. What prompted this?'

'Nothing that I know of, Tony. It just seemed a soothing thing to do. You like cake, don't you? And this one is so prettily decorated, don't you think?'

'Well, yes, it is, but in the shape of a baby? Are we supposed to eat it like that? I'll feel like a cannibal.'

'Oh well, I don't expect you to have it for breakfast.' Hilda put her arms around Tony who was still warm from sleep. 'Let's go back to bed for a little while,' she suggested.

'OK,' replied Tony. Arm in arm, they went back into the bedroom and were both late for work.

Several days later as Hilda walked from the bus-stop towards home, she spotted ahead of her on the pavement the old boyfriend who had appeared in the dream.

'Nick!' she called out, 'Nick!' and ran to catch up with him. 'Hello, it's been such a long time. How are you?'

'Hilda!' Nick exclaimed, 'It's wonderful to see you looking so well. Are you living around here?'

'Yes, I live just around the corner. We must meet for a drink.'

'OK,' said Nick, 'How about right now?'

Hilda had met Nick when they were both at university. They were introduced by mutual friends and had become lovers very quickly. It was the first serious relationship for both of them and they were keen to have partners with whom to enjoy a little sexual experimentation and a few other activities of which students are so fond. They had got along fairly well initially but the problems started when Hilda joined the Women's Union. Nick felt, and said, that she was getting in with 'a bad lot'. He tried to explain to Hilda that the girls in the Women's Union were all either man-haters or so ugly they had to be gay. Hilda, of course, being her grandmother's grand-daughter knew this was wrong but, nonetheless, she was not yet ready to finish with Nick. They were having some very interesting sex and, besides, it was almost the end of term.

One day after a particularly violent argument with Nick, Hilda looked in her diary to see how soon she could escape to a meeting at the Women's Union and further annoy him. She looked at the dates twice, realising that in the flurry of college activities she had not noticed her period was six days' late. Hilda knew immediately that she was pregnant.

She arranged for a termination without telling Nick and refrained from informing him of her condition until the day before she was due to go into the hospital. He had not noticed a thing, but that was not unusual. Like a lot of men, he found female physiology mysterious and tried not to think about it too often. That evening Hilda went to Nick's room and told him what she was going to do.

'What?' said Nick. 'You are going to do what to my baby? I knew I shouldn't have let you join that goddamned Women's Union.'

'You asshole!' shouted Hilda, 'It's my body and, besides, you couldn't have stopped me from joining the Union. I should have dumped you months ago!'

'And if you had done, this stupid thing wouldn't have happened, would it? Weren't you using the stuff that they gave you? I thought that was what you feminists were about, being able to fuck without consequences. What's the point of a Women's Union if you're going to pull this one on us still, eh?'

'You bastard!' Hilda shouted. 'You bastard! Oh, why did I ever sleep with you in the first place? This is it. You'll never see me again, that's for sure!' Hilda walked towards the door.

'You can't do that to my baby, Hilda, don't open that door.'

'I'm going to open this door Nick, and then I'm going to shut it and as far as I'm concerned that's it, case closed.' Hilda opened the door, went through and slammed it behind her. The next day she went into the hospital and when she came out she was a little worse for wear and tear, but, more important to her, no longer pregnant.

Nick did not make a fuss, in fact, he passed Hilda in front of the library a week later without either speaking or looking at her. During the following term they smiled politely at each other from a distance and Hilda continued her life with determination and force, achieving what she wanted and never letting anyone cross her. She did a Master's Degree in Women's Studies and began to work at an advice agency for women in central London. After meeting Tony, she bought a flat with him, and quickly

became notorious on the local building sites for screaming at the builders on the slightest provocation as she
walked by with her head held high and her neatly-ironed
short skirt. Hilda gave neither the pregnancy nor its
bloody end a second thought.

Then she found herself sitting in a pub having a drink
with Nick.

'So,' Hilda said brightly, 'what have you been doing all
these years?'

'Well,' replied Nick with that same smile that Hilda had
once found appealing, 'I finished my degree and became a
chartered surveyor and now I'm married and we have two
children.'

'Oh,' said Hilda, still smiling. 'That's nice. What does
your wife do?'

'She stays at home with the girls. That's the way we
both like it.' Nick sounded a little defensive.

'That's great!' replied Hilda, enthusiastically. 'Do you
get to spend much time with them?'

'Not as much as I'd like. Have you any children Hilda?'

'No, no. Tony and I haven't really had time for children.'

'Oh, so I guess you've learned to use birth control a
little bit better, have you? No more little slip-ups and
rub-outs, eh? Or is he impotent? If I remember correctly
you certainly weren't. You were a randy and fertile little
bitch in the old days, Hilda, a real sex-machine. It's too
bad – that kid would have been very smart but probably
too bolshie in the end, like its mum.'

Hilda sat looking at Nick with slack-jawed amazement.
When he stopped speaking and smiled at her, she picked
up her bulky bag and walked out of the pub. The flat was
empty, so she ran a very hot bath. Sweat formed on her
brow and her upper lip making it difficult to tell which
drops were tears as they plopped off her chin and into the
water.

Hilda sat soaking for a long time, periodically letting

some of the water drain and then refilling the tub with hot water. Her back ached and her breasts were throbbing. She lay back with her eyes closed and tried to keep Nick's words from repeating themselves in her head.

Suddenly, Hilda remembered the dream she had had earlier in the week. She recalled the vine that had twisted up her legs; she remembered being chased. Hilda knew then, with a physical certainty that she had not felt for many years, that she was pregnant.

Getting out of the bath, she stood in front of the mirror speaking to her reflection. 'Not again. I'll lose all my freedom. I'll lose what I've worked for. I'll lose Tony. It will take over my body and I'll get fat and I won't be able to go out in the evenings any more. It'll be nappies and bottles and crying and sleepless nights and no one will ever take me seriously again. I'll have to retire from public life.' She turned around and looked over her shoulder at her back.

'Maybe I want a baby. Maybe it's now or never. I am getting older, after all. My mother had had four children by my age now. And Tony isn't Nick; Tony loves me. Maybe Tony would like a baby. He could teach it Russian and sing "The Internationale" to it at bedtime. We could put it into a nursery so I could go to work. Tony could stay home at night with it.'

Hilda turned again and looked at her body from the side. Pushing out her stomach she tried to imagine how she might look in a few months' time. She wondered if she and Tony could cope with this change. What if the baby turned into a Tory?

After drying her hair Hilda dressed and went into the kitchen to start dinner. She opened the fridge and pulled out a plate upon which lay the remains of the cake she had made only a few days before.

The Micro-Political Party

I remember when politics were real, when men were men and women were feminists, and everybody read semiotics and understood what it meant. Times are different now: none of the old ways exist any longer. Nothing ever happens these days and no one searches for meaning any more. No more leaping naked through the frangipani of rhetoric. Life has become very dull.

I remember when, before politics were made illegal, life was rich with contradiction and dilemma. Everybody had something to be cross about. Now, no one is angry. We are all happy consumers. We all have lots of clothes and get new haircuts as often as we want. If I am feeling unhappy I can go out and buy myself some new shoes, anytime I so desire. We have Style and the authorities say that is enough for anyone. We have more Style than any other nation in the entire world and, the authorities say, that is something of which to be truly proud. Looking good can solve any kind of problem. The economy chugs along, the people are satisfied. We all have plenty of Style and Style is plenty for us.

I remember the old days though, before the Style Party took over in a bloodless designer coup, when everything meant something different to what it does today. In fact I remember, for I am very old, when Roland Barthes was not the brandname of an extremely popular type of bluejean. I cannot, however, remember who or what Roland Barthes actually was. Still, it is enough for now to know that Roland Barthes bluejeans are not what they seem.

I have my doubts though. Perhaps my memory is tricking me into investing more faith than is due to foggy notions of meaning. I was a child at the time of the coup and no one ever speaks of that distant past. I have flashes of memory and it is these that disturb me and lead my thoughts away from Style and on to meaning, even though I know it is quite futile. I remember my mother before she disappeared. She would stand in the kitchen weeping into the washing-up, and singing to herself,

'Where, oh where, have my politics gone? Oh where is my Party today, today?' I would hide beneath her skirt, holding on to her legs, and feel her tremble with frustration and sadness. She would mumble and mutter for hours. 'Politics are gone. The Party is over. Everything is meaningless. Nothing is permitted.' I did not understand this as a child and I do not understand it now. All I know is that there is something about Roland Barthes bluejeans that makes me very uncomfortable and it is not the way that they are cut.

But now I am not so alone. I have met others like me. None as old or with such definite memories but others who have a vague feeling that all is not as it appears. We meet in secret, late on Friday nights, in a derelict warehouse near the river. We sit around and drink wine out of the bottle and make disparaging comments about Life. Sometimes we dance and sometimes, after several bottles, we sing the songs from my childhood, tunes I can remember that were played on the radio before the coup. We sing, 'Ooo-ooo, ooo-yeah, Holiday', and we feel like true revolutionaries, although the supposed religious connotations of this song are beyond us.

We know that we are doing something illegal, outlawed

and Unstylish, the ultimate in anti-social crimes. We know that what we do on Friday nights, from late until much, much later, is form a Party. We know that drinking from late until later is somehow political. I know, because my mother went to the Party, and spoke of the Party. She adorned herself with jewels and smeared bright red lipstick across her lips and went to the Party. I know the Party welcomed her because I remember how she sang and spoke of politics and what the Party meant to her. When we gather together on Friday night, wearing our most Stylish clothes, and drinking ourselves into oblivion, we have made a Party and no one can take that away from us. Except the authorities, of course.

So, we continue dodging our *Face* reading seminars, to meet, drink, dance, and attempt to talk about all sorts of things. We find conversation extremely difficult. Our lives are so narrow and so completely concerned with Style that we are virtually incapable of general discussion and only barely able to manage small talk. But we try, and on a tiny level, we succeed. We are engaging in micro-politics. Ours is the Micro-Political Party. Our motto is 'Revolution is Chic'. We know one day we will be able to throw off the chains of Style and burn our Roland Barthes bluejeans. In the meantime, Friday nights will help us stay calm.

A Brief But Electrical Storm

For no apparent reason whatsoever Clare Smith suffered from intermittent, but chronic, depression. Every once in a while she would feel tempted to cut short her days with some self-destructive act – not suicide or anything as dramatic as that but something that would lose her her job or, worse yet, her friends. She would wake up, very suddenly, and feel a desperate need to cry, wail and maybe even moan. And that is what she would do, without hesitation, all the while wondering why.

'I am a happy woman,' she would say to her friends, 'I lead a happy life. I have a good job where I work with good people. My social life is rewarding and I feel involved with the community in which I live. I like my life and my friends. I am', she'd conclude heartily, 'a happy woman.'

But every couple of months Clare woke up in the middle of the night and felt full of despair, anger, and grief. Often she spent several days feeling this way. Unable to work she cancelled all social engagements and sat at home in her room, drinking endless cups of tea and weeping. Or she continued with her usual routine but at work and socially she was, generally speaking, a misery.

'Oh Clare!' her friends would say, exasperated. 'Whatever is wrong with you today?'

'I don't know,' she wailed. 'If I knew I probably wouldn't feel like this.'

'Here,' they would say patiently, 'have another drink.'

'Haven't you ever been struck down with grief in the middle of an ordinary week for no apparent reason?' Clare asked hopefully.

'No,' they replied in unison. 'Not me.' And Clare would wander home by herself, wiping her nose and eyes and marvelling at the extraordinary equilibrium her friends all seemed so adept at maintaining. A few days later all of this had passed and she would feel happy and healthy again, having almost forgotten her previous mood. And yet, while Clare forgot, her friends did not and there remained in the backs of their minds a small bit of worry left over from Clare's last bout. 'Will she or won't she?' they thought to themselves.

In between these dark moods Clare sailed through her life like a ship in smooth and sparkling water on a clear day. In fact, there was a time when she went for almost a year without encountering a single storm. Her life was so even-keeled that she had almost completely forgotten what it was like to feel even a tiny bit depressed. She became the most solidly happy person that anybody knew. Some people found it alarming, she was so perpetually cheerful and lively. In fact most people like a bit of darkness here or there and are unnerved by too much happiness. Almost all personalities have a *memento mori* embedded somewhere within.

And then late one night after having been the life and soul of a party, Clare woke up suddenly. She sat up with a start. At the foot of her bed stood The Reaper. Clare blinked and when she opened her eyes, it was gone. Her window was open and the curtain billowed out into the room. It was raining heavily outside, a hot summer rain, heavy and portentous. The air was thick and a moment later Clare's room was lit up as lightning flashed nearby. In that flash Clare saw that her room was empty. Darkness

fell again and Clare sank back on to her pillows, overwhelmed with sadness. She felt as though her heart had
just been broken. She felt as though someone very near to
her had just died.

Clare lay on her bed feeling numb and unable to think
clearly. She looked up at her ceiling while the ills of the
world washed over her as the sea washes over a ship-
wreck. As she stared up at the plaster swirls and cobwebs
the ceiling began to change shape. Soon she thought she
could make out a relief map of the world and a moment
later the countries all began to glow brightly, half of them
red, half of them green. The sea shone an intense blue as if
it was about to boil. She stared up with horror until
lightning flashed again and, in an instant, the ceiling was covered with familiar and ordinary plaster
swirls. Her room fell dark, all that was left was
the sound of the rain splashing down, and the rustling
noise of her curtain as it fluttered and undulated in the
wind.

Clare's heart was beating at a frantic pace. 'What is
happening to me?' she thought to herself. She lay on her
bed, on top of the covers, as the breeze sent her papers
skittering around the room and opened and closed the
books she had beside her bed. She stayed like that all
night. When the sky began to lighten near dawn, the
wind died down, the rain slowed to a shower, and the air
no longer felt full of electricity. As the sun came up Clare
dozed off to sleep, waking an hour or so later when her
alarm went off. At the sound of the bell, she opened her
eyes, looking first to the foot of the bed and then up at the
ceiling. She felt slightly calmer although very tired. As the
smell of the coffee brewing in her automatic coffee
machine wafted into the room she sniffed and, with a
shock, felt tears run down her face. Turning over, she
buried her head in the pillow and began to cry. She cried
and cried while the coffee burbled cheerfully in the next
room and when she heard its alarm go she wiped her face

on the back of her pyjama sleeve and went into the kitchen.

Everything looked just as it had the night before. Clare poured herself a cup of coffee and sat at the kitchen table and wept. Tears rolled off her face and on to her pyjamas while she sipped the coffee. In the shower her tears mixed with the hot stream of water. After drying herself and getting dressed, she went down the stairs and out on to the street which had that after-rain freshness which usually made her feel so clean and light-headed. Dragging herself to work, Clare sat at her desk feeling weak and miserable. Her colleagues settled in around her, shuffling their papers and blowing their noses. Gerry, the office jerk, said out loud to no one in particular, 'That was quite a storm we had last night. Was anyone awake for it? I sat up and watched. It seemed right over the city.' Everyone in the office nodded without looking up from their papers and cups of tea. 'My mother says that storms like that, electrical storms, are God's reckoning, um, God's way of expressing his displeasure with the way we are running our lives. She thinks it has something to do with the decline of law and order in our society. God doesn't like it.'

'Do you mean, Gerry,' said Greg, the office smartass, 'that God thinks there should be a greater police presence on the streets?' Greg snickered cynically, looking back down at his work.

'Well, yes, I guess so,' Gerry said nodding and smiling.

'I always thought that if God was a human he'd be Metropolitan Chief of Police,' Greg replied without looking up again. Everyone else in the office shifted uncomfortably in their seats.

Clare could feel her face blushing red. She stood and walked quickly to the ladies' room, where she went into a cubicle, locked the door, sat on the seat and began to cry. She cried so hard that by the time ten minutes had passed she had made herself sick. Despite not having eaten she threw up several times. She knelt on the floor in front of the toilet and watched the tears fall from her face into the basin. She felt unbearably desolate.

After about half an hour one of her co-workers came into the ladies' room and, hearing Clare in a cubicle, banged on the door.

'Clare, is that you? I thought maybe you'd gone off to do some shopping or something. Are you all right?'

'No,' Clare sobbed. That was all she could manage.

'Jesus,' said Susan, 'you sound ill. What's wrong?' Clare moaned. 'Just a minute,' Susan said with concern, 'Just wait while I pee and then I'll get you out of here. We'll put you in a cab and send you home.' A few minutes later Susan's face appeared under the locked door of the cubicle. 'OK sweetie, will you unlock the door?' Clare attempted to lift her hand to the lock but couldn't do it, so Susan crawled under the door.

'Jesus Christ, Clare, you look awful!' she exclaimed. Standing up and pulling Clare with her, she unlocked the door and dragged Clare over to the sink. She splashed her face with cool water and then dried her with a paper hand-towel. It felt rough on Clare's tear-streaked skin and that made her want to cry even harder. 'Come on baby,' Susan said patiently, 'I'll take you home.'

Within an hour Clare was tucked up in her bed with a hot water bottle, a box of tissues, a coldpack on her forehead and the radio on. Susan had made Clare a cup of tea and some toast which she watched her eat before going back to work. Clare listened to Susan's footsteps recede down the stairs outside her flat. She watched the steam from the cup of tea curl up into the air. And then she fell asleep, a deep and dreamless sleep that carried her without emotion into the next day.

When Clare woke up in the morning to the sound of her ever faithful alarm she felt groggy and her eyes were swollen. She could smell the coffee as she went into the bathroom. Shocked by the way her face looked in the mirror she got into the shower and let the hot water massage her body, washing the salt away from her skin. When she had dried herself she combed her hair slowly and thought about the previous two nights and the day wedged between them. Clare felt puzzled. She couldn't quite remember what had happened. She went into her bedroom and put on a dress, thinking hard all the while. Speaking out loud to herself in the mirror she said,

'I went to work, didn't I? There'd been a storm. A nightmare? I was ill. I felt a bit depressed, energyless, anxious. Living in the city is bad for my health.' As hard as she tried, she could not recall much about that night but she felt more relieved than worried. It was as though something was preventing her from remembering; her mind went a certain distance back in time and then stopped, as if facing a wall.

Clare went to work and when Susan asked her about the previous day's drama she found herself saying,

'I saw the Apocalypse late that night and it made me feel ill,' but before those words had time to register with Susan, Clare corrected herself and said,

'It must have been something I ate.' But no one, including Susan, believed her.